For Equals Only

Philosophy of Race

Series Editor: George Yancy, Emory University

The Philosophy of Race book series publishes interdisciplinary projects that center upon the concept of race, a concept that continues to have very profound contemporary implications. Philosophers and other scholars, more generally, are strongly encouraged to submit book projects that seriously address race and the process of racialization as a deeply embodied, existential, political, social, and historical phenomenon. The series is open to examine monographs, edited collections, and revised dissertations that critically engage the concept of race from multiple perspectives: sociopolitical, feminist, existential, phenomenological, theological, and historical.

Titles in the Series

For Equals Only: Race, Equality, and the Equal Protection Clause, by Tina Fernandes Botts
Politics and Affect in Black Women's Fiction, by Kathy Glass
The Habits of Racism: A Phenomenology of Racism and Racialized Embodiment, by Helen Ngo
Philosophy and the Mixed Race Experience, edited by Tina Fernandes Botts
Violence, Race, and Mourning: Beyond the Aesthetics of Memorialization, by Alfred Frankowski
White Self-Criticality beyond Anti-racism, edited by George Yancy

For Equals Only

Race, Equality, and the Equal Protection Clause

Tina Fernandes Botts

LEXINGTON BOOKS
Lanham • Boulder • New York • London

Published by Lexington Books
An imprint of The Rowman & Littlefield Publishing Group, Inc.
4501 Forbes Boulevard, Suite 200, Lanham, Maryland 20706
www.rowman.com

Unit A, Whitacre Mews, 26-34 Stannary Street, London SE11 4AB

British Library Cataloguing in Publication Information Available

Library of Congress Cataloging-in-Publication Data

Names: Botts, Tina Fernandes, author.
Title: For equals only : race, equality, and the equal protection clause / Tina Fernandes Botts.
Description: Lanham : Lexington Books, [2018] | Series: Philosophy of race | Includes bibliographical references and index.
Identifiers: LCCN 2018027532 (print) | LCCN 2018036739 (ebook) | ISBN 9781498501248 (electronic) | ISBN 9781498501231 (cloth : alk. paper) | ISBN 9781498501255 (pbk. : alk. paper)
Subjects: LCSH: Equality before the law--United States. | Race discrimination--Law and legislation--United States. | United States. Constitution. 14th Amendment. | United States. Supreme Court. | Minorities--Civil rights.
Classification: LCC KF4755 (ebook) | LCC KF4755.B68 2018 (print) | DDC 342.7308/5--dc23
LC record available at https://lccn.loc.gov/2018027532

In loving memory of my father

"No State shall make or enforce any law which shall . . . deny any person within its jurisdiction the equal protection of the laws." —The Equal Protection Clause of the Fourteenth Amendment to the United States Constitution

Contents

Note on Stylistic Convention

Throughout this book, as in my previous work, for the most part I will use lowercase letters for all racial terms. In addition I will use the term "racialized" as a synonym for "black" and "African American," and the term "racialized persons" as a synonym for "blacks," "black persons," "black people" and "African Americans." Similarly, I will use the term "nonracialized" as a synonym for "white," and the term "non-racialized persons" as a synonym for "whites," "white persons," "white people" and "persons of exclusively European descent." I prefer the terms "racialized" and "nonracialized" to the more common terms, because they highlight that the groups of persons to which these terms refer have been created by sociocultural forces rather than by biology or other scientific or essentialist forces or parameters. Where a person I am quoting has used another term, I will retain the person's own usage within the quotation. Sometimes, to convey a particular meaning myself, I will simply put the term in quotes, e.g., "white" people. In the rare instances where I retain usage of the terms "black," "African American," or "white" without quotation marks around the term, I will do so for the reason that, in my estimation, a given phenomenon cannot be identified adequately without usage of the term at issue, e.g., Black Nationalism, black codes, white supremacy, or white privilege.

Acknowledgments

So many great people helped me write this book. The greatest inspiration for this book was my grandfather, Nelson S. Burke. "Pops," as we called him, was an intellectual, an educator, and a tireless advocate for the equal treatment of racialized persons. His great grandfather (my great great great grandfather), Alfred Jones, was the first racialized trustee of public schools in the District of Columbia. At a time when the local government found it difficult to pay teachers, Jones used his own money to pay the teachers of schools for racialized children. Jones was influential in starting the Thaddeus Stevens School for racialized children in DC, which eventually evolved into Dunbar High School, named for the poet Paul Laurence Dunbar, and known for its excellent academics. Pops instilled in me a family legacy going back at least as far as Jones that included a sober sense of responsibility to address racial inequality in the United States. Pops introduced me to the writings of Cornel West and was a great admirer of the work of James Baldwin. I would also like to thank Naomi Zack for inspiring me to use philosophy to think about the problem of American racism and for setting a good example of exemplary scholarship in the philosophy of race. I am also grateful to Elizabeth Anderson and Sally Haslanger. Sally introduced me to Liz, and without Liz and the Department of Philosophy at the University of Michigan, Ann Arbor, this book would not have been written. I am grateful to Liz for providing me with the opportunity to think through some of the more complex questions about equality contained in this book in my year of study with her in Ann Arbor. I am also grateful to the University of Michigan Law School for providing me with a forum through which to think through the ideas in chapter 5 of this book, on multiracial racialized persons, in the form of a talk I gave there in 2015. Thanks to Scott Hershovitz, Gabriel Mendlow and the Program in Race, Law and History at Michigan Law. I would also like to thank George Yancy and Jana Hodges-Kluck for including this book in their series on Philosophy of Race. It is a challenge to find a home for interdisciplinary work, particularly work that takes issue with mainstream orthodoxy, and I appreciate both of their support for this project. Finally, I want to thank my husband of eighteen years, J. Michael Botts, and our two children, Teresa and Blake Botts, for supporting my need to lock myself away in my home office for hours on end to write this book in homage to both the ancestors and to the present and future generations of racialized persons in the United States who deserve equal treatment under the law.

Tina Fernandes Botts, Fresno, California, 2018

Introduction

This book is an inquiry into the meaning of the Equal Protection Clause of the Fourteenth Amendment to the United States Constitution on the specific question of how the concepts of race and equality at work in Supreme Court decisions interpreting the Clause have affected the way the Clause has been used, or not used, to combat unconstitutional racial discrimination.[1] The central claim of the book is that the way the Supreme Court currently interprets the Clause—that is, as a vehicle through which to successfully challenge laws or policies that are racially discriminatory per se[2]—problematically relies on a biological concept of race and a legal concept of equality, as opposed to a sociocultural/sociohistorical concept of race and a social concept of equality. My contention is that reliance on these concepts is problematic because doing so (1) is out of step with the purpose of the Clause, (2) is out of step with the contemporary context, and (3) results in an exacerbation, rather than an amelioration, of the state of affairs the Clause was designed to address: the manifest unequal social status of racialized persons that obtained after the abolition of chattel slavery in the United States, and that continues to this day. In support of this contention, the book interrogates the concepts of race and equality at work in various Supreme Court decisions over the years that have interpreted the Fourteenth Amendment, and suggests that, if the Clause is to be used for the purpose it was designed to accomplish (on the specific topic of combatting unconstitutional racial discrimination), i.e., to support the social equality of racialized persons, the Supreme Court may need to change the way it thinks about the concepts of race and equality motivating its interpretation of the Equal Protection Clause.

The upshot of the book is that I recommend a different interpretation of the Equal Protection Clause than the one currently utilized by the Supreme Court. Specifically, I recommend an interpretation that understands the goal of the Clause (again, on the specific topic of racial discrimination) as remedying the unequal status of racialized persons, as a group, that was generated by chattel slavery, perpetuated by Jim Crow, and sustained by the aftermath of both. As part of my recommended change in interpretation, I suggest that the Court switch from thinking about race biologically to thinking about race sociohistorically, and that the Court switch from its current practice of utilizing legal equality as the goal of equal protection law to utilizing social equality.

The original Supreme Court interpretation of the Equal Protection Clause was that it prohibited the unequal treatment of racialized persons (former slaves and their progeny) only. Over the years, there were a total of four main interpretations of the Clause (by my count). However, since the 1978 Supreme Court decision of *Regents of the University of California v. Bakke*, the Court has interpreted the Clause as prohibiting racial discrimination per se, that is, as prohibiting laws or policies that differentiate between persons on the basis of race, regardless of the race of the complainant. Traditionally, the rationale provided for this interpretation has been that differentiation on the basis of race is almost always irrelevant to any legitimate governmental purpose, such that laws that make racial distinctions are presumptively unconstitutional.

The oft-cited root of the rationale for the current interpretation of the Clause is what is known as the "color-blind principle," named after the famous words of Supreme Court Justice John Harlan in the dissent of *Plessy v. Ferguson* (1896): "Our constitution is color-blind" (*Plessy*, 1146). However, according to many constitutional law scholars, including Andrew Kull, "[a] blanket prohibition of racial classifications is impossible to locate in a literal reading of the constitutional text, and it has never been acknowledged by the Supreme Court as a requirement of the 'equal protection of the laws' guaranteed by the Fourteenth Amendment" (Kull 1992, 1). Nevertheless, the color-blind principle was the putative objective of the American civil rights movement. From the 1840s to the 1960s, the mantra of the movement was that the government should not be in the business of sorting people by the color of their skin (ibid.). Moreover, by the mid-1960s, "this once radical idea had become a part of the governing liberal consensus of American political life" (Kull 1992, 2). But, according to Kull and others, once the color-blind principle had taken hold, i.e., once the Civil Rights Act of 1964 became law (outlawing discrimination based on race, color, religion, sex, and national origin, and prohibiting unequal application of voter registration laws, racial segregation in schools, employment, and public accommodations), while *legal equality* had been achieved, it became clear that legal equality was inadequate to address the continuing *social equality* of racialized persons in the United States. Enter race-conscious methods for addressing this continuing social equality, and the backlash thereto in the form of a resurgence in preference for the color-blind principle on the part of the nonracialized majority. Part of this backlash was (and still is) a slew of cases identifying so-called *reverse racism* (racism against nonracialized persons) as not only a real phenomenon, but something the Equal Protection Clause was meant to address.

The current project arose out of a long-standing concern I had ever since law school that the current interpretation of the Clause (that legal equality is the goal of the Clause, as informed by the color-blind principle) was problematic in two key ways. First, the interpretation was out of step with what I have always understood as the purpose of the Clause: namely a vehicle for members of historically marginalized and oppressed groups to challenge and then have struck down laws that perpetuate or exacerbate their unequal social status in society, a status, incidentally, that had been created and perpetuated by oppression.[3] Second, the various Supreme Court decisions interpreting the Clause over the years since the Clause's enactment in 1868, read together, did not seem to me to admit of any sort of consistent or coherent legal doctrine on the question of what is uniquely problematic about racial discrimination such that we need a special constitutional clause to address it. As Andrew Kull has put the problem: "From *Plessy* [*v. Ferguson (1896)*] onward . . . it is impossible to identify in the opinions of the Supreme Court of the United State a constitutional law of racial classifications that may usefully be distinguished from the ad hoc policy preferences of a majority of the Court" (Kull 1992, 5).

In jurisprudence class, I thought I discovered the root of these inconsistencies when I learned about the Critical Legal Studies Movement, a movement in the philosophy of law during the late 1980s and early 1990s, according to which laws have no facial meaning, only the meanings ascribed to them by political actors who come to the interpretation of laws with agendas (however unconscious). Accordingly, from the perspective of Critical Legal Studies, there was actually no definitive meaning of the Equal Protection Clause, or any other law, to be found. Instead, every Supreme Court decision as to what a given law "means" is at bottom a function of politics. Over the almost 150 years since the Fourteenth Amendment to the U.S. Constitution (which contains the Equal Protection Clause) was enacted in 1868, there have been multiple different interpretations of the meaning of the Clause on the topic of how racial discrimination should be handled, jurisprudentially speaking. From a Critical Legal Studies perspective, none of these interpretations is any more credible than any other, such that the current interpretation is as legitimate as any other.

But, could that be all there was to the meaning of the Equal Protection Clause, I asked myself? Was there no way to discern something on the order of a legitimate or authentic interpretation of the Clause on the topic of how racial discrimination should be handled? When Thurgood Marshall stood before the Supreme Court in 1952 to argue in *Brown v. Board of Education* that the only justification for separate schools for children of different races was one that was *constitutionally unsound,* and also designed to keep a people who were at one time slaves as near to that stage, and that level of hobbled autonomy, as possible, was there no credible basis for him to have made that argument? Was there no credible basis for the Supreme Court to have concluded in *Brown* that separate schools were "inherently unequal" under the Equal Protection Clause? The word "separate" just means detached, away from, other than, right? Surely, "separate" does not *inherently* mean unequal. There is no obvious reason why separate schools could not be equal, right?

But, the Supreme Court did not merely say in *Brown* that separate schools for children of different races were unequal *in fact,* leaving open the possibility that separate schools could also have the possibility of being equal. No. Instead, the Supreme Court declared that "separate" schools were *inherently* unequal, i.e., intrinsically unequal or essentially unequal. Leaving aside the philosophical question of whether anything can be inherently any particular way (i.e., leaving aside the question of the possibility of intrinsic valuation), let us examine the question of just what the Supreme Court did, in fact, mean by stating that separate schools were "inherently unequal." It seems to me obvious that the only thing the Court could have meant is that *in the particular sociohistorical context of public school education in the early 1950s in the United States,* separate schools for children of different races were, in virtue of how they were created, what they stood for, and, yes, what they *were,* clearly and manifestly—yes, "inherently"—unequal.

Was this an accident? How did the link happen between "separate" schools and the fact that the schools for children of one racial group were clearly and self-evidently ("inherently") of a lower quality than the schools for children of another racial group? Was it mere chance that caused the schools of racialized children under Jim Crow to be almost always of a lower quality than the schools for nonracialized children? Could it have happened, in other words, that the schools of nonracialized children under Jim Crow had been the ones to have ended up as the "inherently" lower quality schools? In other words, was the mere fact that children of different races were segregated from each other the root cause of the "inherent" difference in quality between the schools of racialized children and the schools of nonracialized children? Was the making of distinctions between children on the basis of race the evil that had to be rooted out and eliminated as a basis upon which to make distinctions between groups of children in public education? Did the mere fact of racialized children's going to school only with each other cause the "inherent" unequal status of their schools? Were racialized children *themselves,* by implication, "inherently" unequal?

It seemed to me in law school (as it seems to me now) that the answer to all of these questions is surely and obviously no. But, it also seems to me that the Supreme Court got it right when it declared in 1954 that separate schools between children of different races were "inherently unequal." I arrive at that conclusion by determining what "inherently unequal" meant *in the context of segregated public schools for children of different races in 1954.* In other words, the "inherent" inequality between schools set aside for children of different races in 1954 was based in the *historical reality* that the schools for racialized children were set up in the first place to maintain social segregation between the descendants of

African slaves, on the one hand, and all other children on the other. Put another way, the separate schools were set up to maintain white supremacy after the Civil War. In other words, the phrase "inherently unequal" means incapable of being equal owing to the long history of marginalization, subjugation, and oppression of racialized people in the United States, and the problem that the Supreme Court had to address in *Brown* was not racial classification per se, but racial classification in that particular context.

The problem in *Brown*, in other words, was not racial classification per se, not the idea of racial classification, and not racial segregation in the abstract, regardless of the races of the children involved. Instead, the problem was that *racialized children* were not getting a quality education *in virtue of the long history in the United States of the oppression of racialized persons*, and all of the socioeconomic, educational, housing, and other social ills experienced by racialized persons that resulted from that oppression, including generations and generations of subpar educational opportunities, employment opportunities, and other social and legal indignities.

How did it happen that American schools were in this state of "inherent" inequality along the color line? What is the story of America's sociopolitical history that necessitated unequal schools along the color line? Was the law complicit in creating this state of affairs? If so, how did the law evolve so as to be complicit? If so, how central has equal protection law been in this process? Has equal protection law weakened or facilitated the inherent inequality of racially segregated school systems? What is equal protection law? What are the political theories at the root and heart of equal protection law? What theories of race, if any, undergird this area of law? What theories of equality undergird it? Why is it the case, over seventy years since the decision in *Brown*, that *public schools in the United States are still inherently unequal along the color line*? If we are in a so-called post-racial society, what is to account for this state of affairs? These are the philosophical questions with which I will try to come to grips in this book.

Perhaps, as some have suggested, it is not the schools but racialized people themselves who are "inherently" unequal. Perhaps the responsibility for the continued inequality of public education along racial lines is rightly placed directly in the hands of racialized persons themselves. But, perhaps neither of these things is the case. Perhaps the explanation for the continued inherent inequality of public schools along racial lines is that the schools are reflective of the continuing effects of institutional racism on the lives and possibilities for full autonomy for racialized people in the United States. Perhaps the vestiges of American slavery are still with us. Perhaps in our haste to put slavery behind us, in our haste to heal the collective shame that is a remnant of having housed that institution for 245 years (1620 to 1865), we have not yet done enough to eliminate those vestiges.

The intent of the book is civil rights reform on the topic of racial discrimination through recommending a reevaluation of the concepts of race and equality at work in equal protection law. Civil rights reform is necessary because, as critical race theorists have been (aptly) pointing out for the last twenty-five years or so, traditional civil rights discourse (according to which, among other things, racism is nothing other than "believing that someone's race is important when it isn't")[4] actually hurts racialized persons more than it helps them. This is because such discourse removes racial discrimination from the daily realities in which it is experienced and abstracts it out to be problematic in principle rather than on the ground in the lives of real people. In so doing, institutionalized racial discrimination becomes illegal wherever and to whomever it occurs (regardless of the race of the would-be victim) rather than in the specific instances in which it operates to perpetuate the long history of the systemic degradation and dehumanization of racialized persons in the United States. Owing to the systemic nature of racial stratification and social privilege based on race in the United States, the belief that racism is nothing other than "believing that someone else's race is important when it isn't" plays out, in the equal protection context, as the recent trend in successful cases of alleged "reverse racism" or cases in which nonracialized persons, more so than racialized persons, are successful when bringing equal protection cases before the Supreme Court.

From a certain vantage point (the vantage point of liberalism and/or liberal legal theory), and perhaps on the surface, the contemporary interpretation of the Equal Protection Clause sounds evenhanded and fair. Racial discrimination is racial discrimination, the argument goes, such that any time race is used as a factor in a public policy or law, that public policy or law is unconstitutional. But, this *ideal* understanding of why racial discrimination is problematic in the United States is out of step with both what race is, and the concept of equality envisioned by the drafters of the Clause. Race is a sociocultural/sociohistorical construct, not a biological fact, both for the drafters of the Clause and according to current academic wisdom. Moreover, the concept of equality driving the drafters of the Equal Protection Clause was social equality rather than the legal equality utilized in contemporary interpretations of the Clause, and the social inequality motivating the inclusion of the Clause in the Fourteenth Amendment is still with us.

In this book, I recommend a different understanding of what the Equal Protection Clause means than the understanding dictated by (ideal) liberal legal theory and with which the U.S. Supreme Court is currently operating. The recommended change in understanding of what the Clause means is rooted in a demonstration that the concepts of race and equality driving recent Supreme Court decisions interpreting the

Equal Protection Clause are hermeneutically off base (that is, out of step with both the original meaning of the Clause and the meaning of the Clause warranted by the contemporary context), resulting in a meaning of the Clause that is incompatible with the goal of the achievement of equality for all, particularly racialized persons. Toward the end of the book, I will engage with recent scholarship on the problems with ideal theory, specifically ideal theory's inability to grapple with racial inequality.[5] I will contextualize the current project as taking place within the critique of liberal legal theory that is contained within that scholarship. The chapter summaries that follow provide more specifics on how the book will proceed.

CHAPTER SUMMARIES

Chapter 1 sets forth the scholarly backdrop of the book. It explains that legal hermeneutics, critical philosophy of race, and Critical Race Theory are the critical lenses through which the problem of legal interpretation that is at the center of the book (i.e., how the Equal Protection Clause of the Fourteenth Amendment to the U.S. Constitution should be interpreted in the twenty-first century as regards racial discrimination) will be explored. The chapter highlights that (1) the key insight of legal hermeneutics is that the question of how a given law should be interpreted is the same question as how that law should be applied, and that (2) the modus operandi of legal hermeneutics is to give as much credence, in the interpretive process, to the sociohistorical context in which a given law is being applied as to the intention of the drafters of the law. The chapter also lays out recent work in critical philosophy of race in which the problem of American racism is examined and interrogated. In this scholarship, theoretical support for the idea that the Equal Protection Clause should be reinterpreted in such a way as to better achieve equality for racialized persons can be found through an insistence that we do not live in a post-racial society, but in a society teeming with racism. The chapter concludes by setting forth key ideas in Critical Race Theory (that branch of jurisprudence that proactively interrogates the relationship between race, racism, and American law) that support and provide a context for the central themes of the book, including a critique of liberal legal theory on the grounds that it does not and very likely cannot grapple with the problem of the persistence of American racism.

Chapter 2 lays out the jurisprudential problem to be addressed in the book, i.e., a less than workable contemporary interpretation of the Equal Protection Clause that currently operates to the advantage of nonracialized persons more often than racialized persons. The chapter contains a description of the current state of equal protection law vis-à-vis racialized persons. It identifies and establishes a core list of seminal and pivotal equal protection cases and analyzes each case in terms of its place in the development of current equal protection law in the area of racial discrimination. The chapter has a historical cast in that it traces the evolution of the relationship between equal protection law and racialized persons from the ratification of the Fourteenth Amendment to the U.S. Constitution in 1868 to the most recent Supreme Court cases that have interpreted the Equal Protection Clause. The goal of the chapter is to establish that while equal protection law originally had as its purpose the protection of members of racialized minority groups from the continued discrimination they faced after the end of the Civil War, equal protection law currently provides little, if any, protection from racial discrimination for such persons. Instead, it operates most often for the protection of nonracialized persons. This is a problem only if the protection of racialized persons from racial discrimination is understood as a key purpose of the Equal Protection Clause. This book certainly takes the position that this is a problem.

Chapter 3 makes the case that the switch on the part of the Supreme Court from understanding the Equal Protection Clause as having been intended to protect racialized persons from racial discrimination to serving the purpose of protecting everyone from "racial discrimination" across the board (that is, regardless of the race of the complainant) is accompanied by a switch on the part of the Court from thinking about race sociohistorically to thinking about race biologically. To make this case, the chapter conducts an investigation into the concept of race at work in equal protection law. An exploration into what the concept of race has been taken to mean by the Supreme Court over the years reveals that while the Court started out thinking of race as a sociocultural/sociohistorical phenomenon, it gradually switched over time to its current position that race is a purely biological phenomenon. During the same time period, the Court switched from thinking of racial discrimination as problematic because it perpetuated the "badges of slavery" (that is, racial discrimination kept racialized persons from many of the rights and privileges of citizenship) to thinking of racial discrimination as problematic per se. Chapter 3 correlates equal protection law's current failure to adequately protect the equality rights of racialized persons with the Supreme Court's shift in thinking about the concept of race from sociocultural to biological. Along the way, the various ways in which the concept of race is understood in the discipline of philosophy will be explained, as well as the American folk conception of race. The point will be made that application of equal protection law to racial discrimination in the abstract, or per se, that is regardless of the race of the complainant (rather than applying equal protection law to the specific case of racial discrimination against racialized persons) is correlated with only nonracialized persons being protected by the law.

Chapter 4 explores the concept of equality at work in equal protection law and argues that over time there was a switch in Supreme Court thinking about what form of equality is at work in the Equal Protection Clause. The point will be made that in early equal protection law, social equality was the focus of equal protection law, whereas in recent Supreme Court decisions, legal equality is the focus. Social equality is at bottom equality of social status, understood as a key component of a society of equals. It is important that social equality is distinct from both equality of outcome and moral equality, although it is similar to both. Legal equality, on the other hand, is theoretically the same as "justice" and/or equal treatment before the law. But, "justice," in the Western tradition, is rooted in Aristotelian proportional equality, according to which equality is available for equals only and not for unequals. Another aspect of Aristotle's theory of justice is that there are "natural" slaves in the world, to whom no equality is due. Chapter 4 will make the case that Aristotle's conception of justice is carried over into the Enlightenment, in the form of Social Contract Theory, and then into the contemporary conception of legal equality. If this is true, then it explains why equal protection law currently operates for the protection of nonracialized persons more than racialized persons, i.e., because the concept of legal equality or "justice" masks the racism and racial inequality that is part and parcel of liberal legal theory more broadly.

Chapter 5 explores the special case of multiracial people in the United States in an effort to highlight the nonsensical nature of treating race as biological in antidiscrimination law (of which equal protection law is one aspect).[6] The special case of multiracial people is helpful for understanding the extent to which the biological concept of race at work in equal protection law undermines equal protection of the laws. Multiracial persons have long been left out of the antidiscrimination law loop as a result of their perceived status as at once belonging to multiple and no particular legally cognized racial group. At the same time, recent scholars of the relationship between multiracial identity and the law have established the long history of hostility toward mixed race persons in the United States, as well as their systematic alienation from the benefits of mainstream antidiscrimination law. Not surprisingly, judicial decisions regarding multiracial persons' right to nondiscrimination are always muddled and internally inconsistent, with the judge(s) writing the decision often switching back and forth between cognizing the multiracial person as first a member of one race and then another, but never both (or all three, or all four as the case may be), that is, never cognizing the multiracial person as a multiracial person. Chapter 5 will make the case that if the language of, and legislative history surrounding, the Equal Protection Clause are to be taken seriously, then equality violations against multiracial persons must also be taken seriously, as must multiracial identity itself. The book will make the case that this can only be accomplished by understanding race sociohistorically rather than biologically generated.

Chapter 6 reflects upon the conclusions derived in the first five chapters. The chapter will place the recommended changes to how the Supreme Court thinks about equal protection law in further dialogue with Critical Race Theory and critical philosophy of race. The chapter speculates on whether changes in the law can help achieve the goal of racial equality and suggests that if such changes in the law can help achieve racial equality, it will only be if Derrick Bell's concept of "interest convergence" is at work.

NOTES

1. I say "unconstitutional" racial discrimination because I think there is also *constitutional* racial discrimination. In other words, as will become clear later in the book, I do not subscribe to the view that differentiating between persons on the basis of race is per se unconstitutional, that is, regardless of the race of the target of discrimination.

2. I define laws or policies that are "racially discriminatory per se" as laws or policies that use race as the criterion of differentiation among persons irrespective of the race of the persons(s) negatively affected by the law or policy.

3. The Equal Protection Clause has also been utilized to successfully challenge laws that perpetuate or exacerbate the unequal status of women, whose unequal status in society, as is the case with racialized persons, was arguably created and perpetuated by oppression. For a sophisticated treatment of how women's unequal status in society was created by oppression, see Cudd 2006.

4. *See* Crenshaw, Gotanda, Peller, and Thomas 1995, xiv.

5. Utilization of the phrase "ideal theory" is a reference to a key aspect of John Rawls's liberal juridicopolitical theory as found in *A Theory of Justice* (1971) and *Political Liberalism* (1996), among other works.

6. I refer to multiracial people as "multiracial racialized people" in chapter 5. I explain why at the top of the chapter.

ONE

Scholarly Backdrop

There are three main areas of scholarly inquiry that form the backdrop of this book and that frame its central questions and methods: legal hermeneutics, critical philosophy of race, and Critical Race Theory.

LEGAL HERMENEUTICS[1]

To some, the argument in this book to the effect that the Equal Protection Clause is properly interpreted, in the current interpretive moment, in keeping with the intentions of the abolitionists who designed the Clause, that is, with special attention to the equality rights of racialized persons, may look a lot like an argument in favor of originalism, or the idea that the original intent of the Framers or drafters of the Constitution should be controlling on the question of the meaning of the Constitution, when making decisions as to how the Constitution and its various components and clauses should be interpreted or applied today. There is validity to this observation, to a certain extent. That is, it is certainly the case that one goal of this book is to call attention to the intent of the abolitionists who drafted the Equal Protection Clause, and who lobbied to include it in the Fourteenth Amendment. However, unlike for originalists, the intention of the Framers or drafters is not dispositive on the question of the meaning of the Constitution for those, like myself, who subscribe to a legal hermeneutical approach to constitutional meaning. What must also be considered, from a legal hermeneutical point of view, is, among other things, the context of the present situation in which the particular constitutional clause or article is being applied.

Legal hermeneutics as a theory of constitutional interpretation can be traced back to the publication of Francis Lieber's nineteenth-century work, *Legal and Political Hermeneutics* (Lieber 1880/2010). There, Lieber tried to identify principles of legal interpretation that would bring consistency and objectivity to the interpretation of the U.S. Constitution (Mootz 1992, 117) while at the same time exposing strict intentionalist interpretative methods as incoherent (Binder and Weisberg 2000, 48).[2] Over 125 years after Lieber's landmark text, contemporary legal hermeneutics in constitutional theory retains Lieber's goal of objectivity of interpretation, as well as his attention to the roles of history, temporality, politics, and sociohistorical context in any attempt to "understand" a legal text.

The question of the nature of legal interpretation is central to constitutional theory. As many scholars of jurisprudence have observed, before we can decide what the constitution means, we must first decide the best interpretive method. The choice of method is constrained to a large extent for a given theorist by where that theorist fits on a methodological continuum between two loosely defined but fundamentally opposed approaches to constitutional interpretation that can be called for purposes of the present discussion "originalism" and "non-originalism."[3] Originalism is the view, generally, that the meaning of the constitution is to be found by determining the original intent of the Framers, understood to be most prudently found in the text of the constitution itself.[4] By contrast, non-originalism is the view, generally, that the constitution is a "living, breathing document" intended more as a set of guidelines for future lawmakers than as a strict rulebook demanding literal compliance.

In the realm of constitutional theory, legal hermeneutics is unique and somewhat revolutionary in that it not only refuses to align itself with either pole on the methodological continuum between originalism and non-originalism, it goes one step further and rejects the continuum itself as wrong-headed.[5] Indeed, legal hermeneutics rejects interpretive method altogether in favor, instead, of a call to an increased level of self-reflexivity on the part of the interpreters of laws meant to actively and consciously account for the role of the interpreter (and of interpretation) in meaning-generation in a way that neither originalism nor non-originalism is able to accommodate.[6]

A legal hermeneutical approach to constitutional interpretation, then, calls the interpreter of the constitution to consciously recognize the roles of the identities of the drafters and interpreters of laws, the identity of the original author, the sociohistorical context in which the text was originally written, the sociohistorical context in which the (current) interpretation is taking place, the political climate at the time the text was written, the political climate in which the (current) interpretation is taking place, *the extent to which the meaning of words and concepts relevant to the interpretation have changed or have not changed over time, the particularity of experience of those affected by a given law*, the extent to which that experience is acknowledged or unacknowledged by previous interpretations, and various other factors which legal hermeneutics takes to necessarily affect the quality of the communicative enterprise between the interpreters of laws and the legal text in any attempt to understand or determine the "meaning" of the Constitution, or parts of the Constitution.

The work of George H. Taylor is at the vanguard of contemporary legal hermeneutics within the realm of jurisprudence proper. George Taylor's work in legal hermeneutics follows Ricoeur's in philosophical hermeneutics. In his "Hermeneutics and Critique in Legal Practice," Taylor argues that Ricoeur's approach to hermeneutics gets it right when it attempts to mediate the difference between understanding and explanation (Taylor 2000, 1101 et seq.). Understanding, on this view, is obtained through hermeneutic methods, but explanation is obtained through science. Ricoeur, according to Taylor, sees the interpretive enterprise as containing both elements. The way Taylor sees it, Ricoeur's emphasis on the narrative nature of meaning acknowledges the roles of both understanding and explanation in a successful interpretation (1123). The usefulness of legal hermeneutics, for Taylor, is that it correctly identifies and brings to the forefront that there is explanation/fact in understanding/interpretation and there is understanding/interpretation in explanation/fact—shedding a kind of glaring light on all "understandings" that might deny this reality. The goals of originalism, on this view, are simply impossible to reach.

Francis J. Mootz III agrees with Taylor about the impossibility of our ability to ascertain the "original" meaning. Accordingly, instead of engaging in what he understands as the necessarily fruitless exercise of attempting to ascertain original meaning, Mootz argues, we should instead attempt to find the interpretation that "allows the text to be most fully realized in the present situation" (Mootz 1988, 605). David Hoy's take on legal hermeneutics involves a focused critique of the "intentionalist" position in constitutional theory, according to which the so-called "intent of the framers" is the ultimate authority on constitutional meaning (Hoy 1992). For Hoy, while the intentionalist believes that no interpretation is needed to locate the intent of the framers, the hermeneuticist understands that the concept of intended meaning presupposes a prior understanding of "meaning" in a different sense of the word. The concept of an ambiguous sentence highlights this prior understanding of "meaning." A given sentence can have two different "meanings" in this prior sense, Hoy explains, whether either or both of them were "intended" or not (175). The hermeneuticist acknowledges, in other words, according to Hoy, a difference between sentence meaning and speaker's meaning. However, while the intentionalist incorrectly presumes that there are only two possible bases for a theory of meaning, intention and convention (ibid.), the hermeneuticist understands that there can be no fact of the matter vis-à-vis sentence meaning. Hoy writes,

> [Hermeneutics] acknowledges semantic complexity. It does not exclude questions about intention when these are relevant to interpretation, but it believes that since textual meaning is not reducible to intended meaning, there are many other kinds of questions that can be asked about texts. (Hoy 1992, 178)

At the same time, Hoy's hermeneutics stands for the proposition that the traditional way that law is practiced operates as a constraint on judicial discretion, it provides a schema of intelligibility in which a judge must necessarily decide a case. As Hoy indicates, using discretion to decide what the law means within the tradition of the practice of law is what judges do all the time. "Only when the judges know that the law entails one decision and they nevertheless decide something else could they be said to be rewriting," writes Hoy (1992, 183), and the hermeneutic claim is that this is almost never the case.[7] If Hoy is right, then there is no act of judicial interpretation that takes place without interpretation. Such a possibility is an illusion. Instead, all acts of "understanding" are acts of interpretation including originalist and/or intentionalist acts of understanding.

The claim that every Supreme Court decision is an act of interpretation, however, is not a claim about the indeterminacy of meaning itself, but a more modest claim about the impossibility of ascertaining original meaning. The difference between these two positions is subtle but important. While for the non-originalist the possibility of authoritative meaning is an illusion, for the legal hermeneuticist authoritative meaning exists and is a function of the interpreter's taking conscious account of several key factors which inform and shape the interpretive process. Taking conscious account of each of these factors when attempting to interpret a given legal text lends to the interpretative process a sort of legitimacy and authority the possibility of which most non-originalist positions deny, together with a level of objectivity (or quasi-objectivity) not achievable or even possible through mainstream interpretive methods.

Legal hermeneutics, then, can be understood as an anti-method in constitutional theory. As Gregory Leyh has, I think correctly, identified, "[h]ermeneutics neither supplies a method for correctly reading texts nor underwrites an authoritative interpretation of any given text, legal or otherwise" (Leyh 1992, xvii). Instead, "the activity of questioning and adopting a suspicious attitude toward authority is at the heart of hermeneutical discourse. Hermeneutics involves confronting the aporias that face us, and it attempts to undermine, at least in partial ways, the calm assurances transmitted by the received views and legal orthodoxies" (ibid.).

Accordingly I hope to show in this book that the contemporary context mandates the same interpretation of the Equal Protection Clause as the one contemplated by the drafters of the Clause, i.e., the Clause should be used to address and help ameliorate the manifest inequality of racialized persons (and not to combat racial discrimination per se) for the reason that the problem the Clause was designed to address—social inequality along racial lines in the United States—persists. The needs of the contemporary context, in other words, i.e., the persistence of racial inequality, necessitate that we use the Clause to address that inequality, rather than to advance the interests of members of the ruling class through using it to address such things as "reverse discrimination."

CRITICAL PHILOSOPHY OF RACE

Critical philosophy of race is philosophical engagement with the concepts of race and racism, as well as issues raised by these concepts. Theoretical support for the idea that the Equal Protection Clause should be reinterpreted in such a way as to better achieve equality for racialized persons can be found in the work of a number of contemporary critical philosophers of race concerned with the continuing unequal status of racialized persons in the United States

Charles Mills, for example, opens *The Racial Contract* with the following statement, "White supremacy is the unnamed political system that has made the modern world what it is today" (Mills 1997, 1). Mills continues by writing that the nonracialized persons who, for the most part, write the standard textbooks and teach the standard courses in political theory "take their racial privilege so much for granted that they do not even see it as *political*, as a form of domination" (ibid.). Moreover, according to Mills, "[p]hilosophy has remained remarkably untouched by the debates over multiculturalism, canon reform, and ethnic diversity racking the academy," adding that, "both demographically and conceptually, it is one of the 'whitest' of the humanities" (2). The way to remedy this situation, according to Mills, is to develop a "global theoretical framework for situating discussions of race and white racism, and thereby challenging the assumptions of white political philosophy" (ibid.). Certainly, the current project is meant to operate in the service of the development of such a "global theoretical framework."

The Social Contract, the cornerstone of liberal political theory, for Mills, obfuscates the "ugly realities" of group power and domination, and in fact, provides a "profoundly misleading" account of the way the modern world actually is and came to be (3). To remedy this state of affairs, Mills develops his Racial Contract, meant as a "conceptual bridge" between the mainstream political theory of nonracialized persons and the political thought of racialized persons. Whereas the mainstream political philosophy of nonracialized persons is concerned with questions such as what justice is and what rights are *in the abstract*, the political thought of racialized persons is concerned with issues of conquest, imperialism, colonialism, white settlement, land rights, race and racism, slavery, Jim Crow, reparations, apartheid, cultural authenticity, national identity, indigenism, Afrocentrism, and similar concerns.

The Racial Contract is Mills's way of explaining the actual genesis of Western (European) civilization and the state, the way Western societies are structured, the way Western governments function, and the moral psychology of the Western mind. The Racial Contract is therefore a corrective on the Social Contract, a modified version thereof, that proactively acknowledges and explains the roles of race and racism in the development of the Western way of life. Mills's Racial Contract is a mechanism or device through which the non-ideal nature of Western society is described and explained, particularly vis-à-vis the mechanism of racial domination contained in Western societies. Mills's point is that the Racial Contract may be a more explanatory theoretical model for understanding the history of Western civilization than the Social Contract, mired as it is in Enlightenment abstractions such as freedom and autonomy, without grappling with the ways in which these ideals work differently for racialized persons than for nonracialized persons, in the real world in which we live.

In keeping with Mills's sentiments in *The Racial Contract,* it is a thesis of this book that the contemporary, standard interpretation of the Equal Protection Clause, like Mills's Racial Contract, operates in the service of the interests of nonracialized persons, as a group, to the detriment of the rights of racialized persons. The interpretation is a form of ideology that operates to mask an ugly reality of racial domination that runs throughout mainstream liberal legal theory. It is a further thesis of this book that this state of affairs has been heavily influenced by two of the key concepts informing and shaping Western liberal juridicopolitical theory: biological race and legal equality.

Derrick Darby has a different take on the problem of racial inequality in America, however. In *Rights, Race, and Recognition,* Darby's primary focus is on the problems of race and racism in the United States, and with the relationship between race and racism and presocial (or "natural") rights. Darby offers us the stark observation that *racialized persons actually have no natural or presocial rights at all,* including a right to equality (Darby 2009). Instead, all rights, for Darby, are bestowed on us by society, that is, generated through social relations. Any so-called right that is not recognized by society is not a right at all, for Darby. If there are presocial rights, Darby seems to be asking, why have they not been acknowledged and realized for racialized persons in the United States? What would it take for presocial rights, if they exist, to be realized for racialized persons in a liberal state, Darby asks us? Some believe that all the liberal state need do is live up to its ideals (of equality for all, etc.) to effectuate the realization of presocial rights. But, some are of the view that the only way to achieve the effectuation of presocial right (if they exist) is for racialized persons is to abandon rights-based liberalism altogether.

Darby explains that many critical race theorists (most, if not all, of whom are racialized persons as well as legal scholars) are concerned that presocial (or "natural") rights actually reinforce and authenticate oppressive social and legal systems and relations. From this point of view, racial oppression stems not from intentional, openly hostile contempt on the part of nonracialized persons, but from the advantages that come from being nonracialized (i.e., from white privilege). Within the oppressive social and legal systems created by nonracialized persons for the benefit of nonracialized persons (i.e., within Charles Mills's Racial Contract), *racial inequality is rendered a perfectly natural state of affairs,* a product of choices made by free and equal individuals. There is no way to effectuate racial equality, for Darby, within the existing liberal legal system. For Darby, then, a rejection of prosocial (or "natural") rights in favor of a world composed entirely of social rights, highlights for our consideration that we may need to change the social world we have created in order to effectuate equality for racialized persons rather than waiting for nonracialized persons to stretch beyond the privileges attendant to their racial status in order to acknowledge the alleged presocial rights of those less privileged.

Areas of the social world particularly in need of change are, for Darby, health care, the criminal justice system, and education. Importantly, for Darby, the liberal tradition (and its classic natural rights doctrine) will not and cannot work to achieve racial equality. It has not worked so far, Darby emphasizes. Moreover, the history of the United States holding both liberal legal theory and chattel slavery for racialized persons at the same time, as well as holding both liberal legal theory and Jim Crow, bears out that the concept of presocial or "natural" rights seems to be perfectly compatible with racial inequality rather than antithetical to it.

Darby's concern that the concept of presocial (or "natural") rights is not helpful in achieving racial equality is echoed in my concern in this book that the anachronistic concept of biological race and liberalism's concept of legal equality are also not helpful in achieving racial equality. In the same way that Darby's presocial rights are an antiquated relic of days gone by that appear to do no real good to help the unequal status of racialized persons in the United States, even serving to obfuscate rather than solve the real equality challenges faced by racialized persons, so the Supreme Court's biological race and legal equality are similarly antiquated and ideological. Better to abandon these concepts outright than continue to try to work against the sociocultural/sociohistorical baggage they carry, and that insidiously prevent us from remembering what the real problem is that the Equal Protection Clause was meant to solve: the manifest and continuing social inequality of racialized persons in the United States.

Tommie Shelby disagrees with Darby's scathing criticism of liberal legal theory's ability to address the problem of continuing racial inequality. In *We Who Are Dark*, Shelby states that he would not abandon liberalism, but offers instead what he thinks is a way to reconcile liberalism and racial equality (Shelby 2005). There, Shelby makes the case that progress can be made to improve the unequal status of racialized persons within the liberal tradition through reconciling that tradition with Black Nationalism. The liberal tradition and Black Nationalism can be reconciled, for Shelby, if the solidarity that Black Nationalism requires to achieve political ends takes place not just between and among racialized persons, but also between racialized persons and nonracialized persons who are sympathetic to the cause of addressing the problems faced by the racialized. The key to such solidarity, for Shelby, is that all parties share what Shelby calls "political blackness," or a desire to end racism, improve conditions for racialized persons in the areas of education and employment, and maintain tolerance for group differences and individuality.

At the start of the book, Shelby states that he thinks racialized persons should hold on to their racial identity as a basis for political solidarity, cultural identity, and group self-realization. This is the case despite recent "attacks" that such a view lacks empirical adequacy, analytical cogency, moral legitimacy, and political significance. To support his view, Shelby takes up the task of defending the idea of race through a critical examination of the normative and conceptual ground of the political culture of racialized persons. For Shelby, racial solidarity has a place and value in contemporary society. As a contribution to the collective project of many contemporary racialized intellectuals to reconceive racialized politics so as to modernize the objectives and strategies of racialized freedom struggles for the post–civil rights era, Shelby advocates for solidarity among racialized persons while at the same time leaving behind racial essentialism. Acknowledging the diversity within the black American population, Shelby's basis for group solidary is political and not natural. One can be in solidarity with racialized persons, for Shelby, i.e., one can share in "political blackness" if one is committed to defeating racism, eliminating unjust racial inequalities, or dedicated to improving the material life prospects of racialized persons, especially the most disadvantaged.

For Shelby, race is an emancipatory tool. He maintains he can hold this conception of racial solidarity while simultaneously rejecting racial essentialism and identity politics. Shelby's project is not as much concerned with who racialized persons are as a people as with the ways in which racialized persons continue to be unfairly treated. Key to Shelby's project is his view that racism still negatively affects the life prospects of racialized persons in the United States and therefore racial justice has not yet been achieved. At the same time, Shelby is optimistic, unlike critical race theorists in the tradition of Derrick Bell, that racism against racialized persons is not permanent. He thinks racialized persons (and those who share "political blackness") can work together to effect meaningful social change. One of Shelby's primary targets, however, is liberals.

While liberals often portray Black Nationalists as divisive, fanatical, dangerous, unprincipled, racist, delusional, and "even mad," for Shelby there is a strand of Black Nationalism that is compatible with liberalism, holding as valuable things like equal citizenship for all persons; respect for individual autonomy; democratic constitutional government under the rule of law; freedom of conscience, expression, and association; tolerance for different conceptions of the good; equal opportunity in education and employment; and the guarantee of a minimum standard of living. This strand of Black Nationalism, for Shelby, then, "has a role to play in helping to realize these liberal ideals" (Shelby 2005, 6). To facilitate compatibility with liberal values, Shelby "rethinks" Black Nationalism so as to, in his mind, make it compatible with political liberalism. At the same time, Shelby argues that his revitalized form of Black Nationalism is also compatible with certain Marxist strands (particularly "Black Marxists") who desire to get "orthodox Marxists" to take the experiences of racialized persons seriously.

Still, Shelby wants to distinguish his revitalized Black Nationalism from Black Marxist traditions, while at the same time aligning his views with Black Radicalism. A focus on class differentiation within the community of racialized persons and on the nature of racist ideology (in the Marxist sense) require a reworking of Black Nationalism, for Shelby, in order to take these phenomena into account. Moreover, Shelby's "proto-nationalism" would leave behind any vestiges of confining women to subordinate ("supporting") roles. "This book assumes as a basic premise that no viable and principled black political solidarity can exist if black women and black men do not treat each other as equals," Shelby writes (2005, 8). Somewhat impressively, Shelby adds that the particular concerns of racialized women would be taken just as seriously as those of racialized men, under his new, revitalized Black Nationalism.

In describing the necessity for racial solidarity, Shelby speaks poignantly of Du Bois and his "pan-African vision" (Du Bois 1995, 117) that includes everyone of African descent (Shelby 2005, 244). At the same time, Shelby narrows his discussion in *We Who Are Dark* to focus on American racialized unity. Regarding the Du Boisian vision, Shelby writes, "Nonetheless, what is important to notice here is that Du Bois grounds his Pan-African vision not in a thick collective identity . . . but in *the common experience of racial injustice and the stigma of being racialized as 'black.'*" Shelby explicitly envelops this Du Boisian vision of the key component of racialized solidarity, into the Black Nationalism he defends. What holds the mutual identification of racialized persons together, for Shelby, is, at least in part, the shared experience of racism against racialized persons. To combat that racism successfully, for Shelby, it is "crucial" that racialized persons work together to maintain a "vigorous character" in support of self-respect and collective self-defense (Shelby 2005, 245).

The form of group identity for racialized persons Shelby endorses he calls "political blackness." According to political blackness, racialized persons who would qualify for group membership should adhere to certain political principles, including antiracism, equal educational and employment opportunity, and tolerance for group differences and individuality. They should also be committed to certain "emancipatory goals" such as achieving substantive racial equality (particularly regarding employment, education, and wealth), and ending ghetto poverty. In short, anyone who stands firm in resistance to the oppression of racialized persons and is firmly committed to racial justice would qualify as racialized, on this view.

Finally, Shelby is on board with self-determination for racialized persons (a traditional piece of Black Nationalism) as long as it does not entail racial essentialism and is compatible with respect for intragroup differences, such as gender, sexuality, ethnicity, nationality, and religion. Such determination is necessarily collective, for Shelby, however, since it is "simply a strategy for resisting, defending against, and overcoming racial oppression" (Shelby 2005, 253). The self-determination of racialized persons, for Shelby, does not advocate or seek separatism, however. Instead, it seeks freedom from racism, relief from the burdens of racial inequality and ghetto poverty, and greater political participation in public life.

In the Shelbian vein this book attempts to reconcile liberalism with an attempt to address the inequality of racialized persons. Whereas Shelby attempts to do that through proposing a kind of black solidarity that does not exclude nonracialized persons as long as they are "down with the program," so to speak, this book does so through a reinterpretation of one of the key features of the civil rights movement, the Equal Protection Clause of the Fourteenth Amendment. Arguably, any attempt to address the problem of racial inequality through a change in the law is a part of the liberal program. On the other hand, however, the particular changes recommended are in keeping with key features of the somewhat radical Critical Race Theory movement, including protesting that race is not an "immutable" (biological) trait but an artifact of hundreds of years of institutionalized (racial) oppression that has as yet seen no end, and exposing the concept of (liberal) equality currently at work in Supreme Court decisions surrounding the Equal Protection Clause as deeply antithetical to and inhibitive of the social equality of racialized persons.

In keeping with her seminal article, "What Is the Point of Equality?" in which Elizabeth Anderson argues that the point or goal of equality is the creation of a "community of equals" based on equal respect for all (a form of social equality) (Anderson 1999), in *The Imperative of Integration,* Anderson explains how she thinks we, as a society, can get there, and that is through forced racial integration (Anderson 2010). For Anderson, neither conservative claims about the cultural pathology of racialized persons nor color-blind liberalism accurately explain the continued inequities faced by racialized persons. In her view, just as segregation is the primary cause of the current state of social inequality, the reverse, or forced integration, is the solution. For Anderson, a revival of a focus on racial integration will ameliorate the injustice and inequality still plaguing racialized communities. Finally, multiculturalist approaches to group differences (basically tolerance) are similarly weak in explanatory or ameliorative power, for Anderson. Instead, for Anderson, we need forcible integration through race-conscious policies and programs to achieve the ideal of equality for racialized persons in the United States. Anderson bases her argument on evidence obtained from the social sciences, including information from economics, sociology, and psychology, making a decidedly empirical case for her "imperative."

Certainly, Anderson's "point" of equality—the creation of a community of equals, i.e., equal dignity and accord for all, or social equality—is a value contained in the current project. If not the point of equality itself, it is certainly a contention of this book that social equality was, and is, the "point" of the Equal Protection Clause. I also share Anderson's sober and serious concern for the persistent social inequality of racialized persons in the United States, and am sympathetic to the urgency she feels that something needs to be done about it. I certainly think race-conscious programs will be helpful toward the achievement of racial equality in the United States, but I am not sure Anderson's imperative of integration fits within Critical Race Theory or critical philosophy of race goals. Although the preservation of group identity is not a priority of the current project, it is certainly not *not* a priority, if the preservation of group identity will help achieve racial equality; and one challenge faced by integration is the prospect of the loss of group identity.

In keeping with this train of thought, Anderson finds tough criticism in Howard McGary's ideas in "Racial Integration and Racial Separatism: Conceptual Clarifications" (McGary 1983/1999). There, McGary compares the integrationist and separatist solutions to the problem of the continuing unequal status of racialized persons in the United States, and despite protestations to neutrality, comes out pretty strongly on the side of separatists. McGary assumes at the outset that there are races and, in particular, that there are racialized persons, and narrows his discussion to the identification of common goals of both integrationists and separatists, the identification of where the goals and ideals of integrationists and separatists diverge, and the making of an assessment as to where these similarities and differences "leave us" in terms of resolving the problem of the continuing unequal status of racialized persons in the United States.

A key common goal of both groups, for McGary, is the elimination of the problems confronting racialized persons as a group.[8] But, the integrationists and separationists disagree about *what the problems are in the first place* and *how to solve them*. Most integrationists, for example, seek to integrate racialized persons into the culture of nonracialized persons on the reasoning that most nonracialized persons enjoy advantages and opportunities that racialized persons do not enjoy, such that if racialized persons become more like nonracialized persons, the disadvantages and inequalities would be eliminated. The assumption contained in this solution to the problem of continuing inequality for racialized persons is that there is something about the culture of racialized persons that is causing the inequality. Most cultural and economic separatists disagree. In their view, this approach to the elimination of the continuing inequality of racialized persons will not work, since there is no evidence that the culture of nonracialized persons ("the white Anglo-Saxon ideal") is a good model for defining social arrangements, or providing solutions to the problems racialized persons face.

Another ideological difference between integrationists and separatists, for McGary, is "the belief by the integrationist that [the integrationist] is entitled to judge what is best for all people [regardless of their race]" (56). The separatist, by contrast, does not feel entitled or obligated to define appropriate strategies for races other than his or her own. The separatist reasons that a person of one race does not have the information or shared experiences to know what members of another race need or how their needs ought to be met.

Moreover, unlike the integrationist, the separatist rejects the ideal of individualism, and endorses collectivism, believing that one of a person's primary obligations is to the racial group of which the person is a member. "All racial or cultural separatists," according to McGary, "put the interest of racialized persons as a cultural and racial group before their own personal welfare and, of course, before the welfare of other groups" (57).

Despite facially refusing to take a side on the divide between integrationists and separatists, McGary's preference for the separatist position is evident in the article. "African-American and white communities are a reality everywhere in the United States," writes McGary. "The policy maker should not ignore this reality," he continues (58). "It has not been demonstrated that equality, fairness, or justice require that we eliminate these communities," McGary concludes (58). The separatist solution? The resources of racialized persons should be expanded so that they can be in a position to meet their own needs, which, in addition to meeting their more tangible (economic) needs, will also result in a healthy self-concept based on having control over their own lives. A key theme in separatist solutions to the problems faced by racialized persons, control over their own lives (also known as *group autonomy*), is not a theme that can be found in integrationist literature, according to McGary. McGary writes, "Integrationists appear to believe that there is no point in having control if this does not promote one's welfare in regard to the basic necessities of life" (68). Separatists, on the other hand, according to McGary, "do not believe that the welfare or good self-esteem of [racialized persons] can be fully secured unless [racialized persons] have control over their lives" (58).

In summary, for McGary, integrationists prioritize improving the welfare of racialized persons over group self-determination, whereas separatists prioritize group self-determination over welfare. But, the real questions, according to McGary, are (1) whether the emphasis on welfare over self-determination will eliminate the subjugation of racialized persons and promote better race relations, (2) whether group self-determination is a necessary condition for individual racialized persons to enjoy certain basic rights that are taken for granted by most nonracialized Americans, and (3) whether trying to eliminate racial distinctions altogether (or keeping them and playing down their importance) is the best way to promote good race relations. McGary does not take an official position on these questions, but his preference for separatism is clear. I certainly share in McGary's apparent preference for self-determination over welfarism; and I also share his concern that the liberalism grounding integrationism is without the resources to address the unique problems faced by racialized persons. One of the hoped outcomes of my suggestions to changing the way equal protection law operates is to place the tool of the Equal Protection Clause back in the toolbox of racialized persons themselves, so as to facilitate their own self-empowerment. In other words, if racialized persons can once again use the Equal Protection Clause to have laws and policies struck down that inhibit the autonomy to which they are entitled as citizens, integration as a solution to racial equality may seem less "imperative" on the path to racial equality. I also share, as will be made more clear later in the book, McGary's concern that integrationism (as a form of liberal legal theory) is *without the resources* to address the specific equality needs of racialized persons.

In *Black Bodies, White Gazes,* George Yancy grapples with the problem of the social inequality of racialized persons through demonstrating the way in which racialized persons continue to be seen, experienced, and processed by nonracialized persons in disturbing ways (Yancy 2017). Among Yancy's claims are that (1) nonracialized persons regularly interact with racialized persons with hatred, disgust, and fear, denying the subjectivity of racialized persons and creating an almost insurmountable polarization between racialized and nonracialized persons, (2) the status of nonracialized persons in society is a function of differentiating themselves from racialized persons, (3) nonracialized persons see themselves as individuals but see racialized persons as types, (4) racialized persons are rendered problematic within the systems of domination and subordination created by the way in which racialized persons are processed by nonracialized persons, with nonracialized persons seeing themselves as the standard by which everyone and everything else is measured, (5) racialized persons must organize resistance to domination by nonracialized persons in order to maintain some sense of identity, dignity, and agency within these systems, (6) what it means to be a racialized person is learned through experiencing the social ramifications of being racialized within the systems of meaning and domination created by nonracialized persons, and (7) since it is difficult for nonracialized persons to put an end to the systems of domination from which they benefit, it is incumbent on nonracist nonracialized persons to change the way that nonracialized persons, in general, see and interact with racialized persons.

Yancy's detailed account of the lived experience of racialized persons goes a long way toward establishing the kind of social inequality the Equal Protection Clause was designed to help ameliorate. Without testimony such as is contained in this book, the nature of the distinctive kind of social inequality experienced by racialized persons arguably remains invisible to nonracialized persons, who, in virtue of their privileged status in society, never (or extremely rarely) have firsthand experience with racial inequality. Moreover, Yancy captures well the almost innocent way in which racism operates in contemporary society. I say "almost" innocent, because from a certain political point of view, we are all (even the privileged among us) responsible for educating ourselves on the proper and respectful ways to interact with those who are different from ourselves, and none of us is "innocent" who engage, however inadvertently, in the perpetuation of institutionalized oppression. However, as Yancy's book makes clear, most nonracialized persons actually *have no clue* about the degree to which the way they function in the world operates to perpetuate racial inequality and oppression. This is as true in Yancy's elevator (where the nonracialized often cower in fear in the presence of racialized persons) as it is in the chambers of the Supreme Court. As Yancy highlights, it is no longer the sheet-wearing monster who metes out racial inequality and oppression, but the juridicopolitical machine of liberalism, the (conscious or subconscious) racist ideology it entails, and the (conscious or unconscious but, in any event, racially motivated) damaging actions taken by the members of that machine.

Trying to address this reality, in *The Color of Our Shame,* Chris Lebron asks, "How is it that forty years after the passage of the Civil Rights Act and relative disappearance of explicit racism can we account for the continued marginalization of blacks and black identity?" (Lebron 2013, 2). Lebron continues, "[W]hile we no longer publicly hang blacks by the neck, the fact of systemic racial inequality poses an existential threat all the same for it indicates America's lack of consistency to the ideal of moral equality, which has real costs for black lives" (ibid.). Writes Lebron, "Stated succinctly, systemic inequality consistently and persistently diminishes the ability of blacks to conceive and/or pursue a good life" (ibid.). For Lebron, "we" (American society) know better (we have the appropriate and necessary ideals in place), but we rarely and inconsistently *do* better. America has a bad character, Lebron argues, and it is not taking the appropriate steps to rectify the situation. The social reality is that racial inequality endures, by which Lebron means "the basic phenomenon that blacks are not receiving as much of something as whites. That may be wealth or opportunity or resources broadly construed" (Lebron 2013, 3). Once we add the word "systemic" to "racial inequality," says Lebron, we acknowledge that this inequality is not discrete or unique or isolated but pervasive. But, for Lebron the word "systemic" also removes the intentionality from the problem as well. Systemic racial inequality is present but not (or no longer) deliberate. Instead, Lebron argues that the problem of racial inequality is *the problem of social value,* which Lebron describes as the reality that racialized persons simply "do not occupy an equal place in the scheme of normative attention and concern upon which our society depends in the first place to justify the distribution of benefits and burdens as well as to identify those who are deserving or appropriate recipients" (Lebron 2013, 4). America cannot improve its bad character or address its systemic racial inequality, in other words, for Lebron, until it first decides that racialized persons are equal in social value to nonracialized persons, that is, deserving of an equal place "in the scheme of moral attention."

Lebron does an excellent job of describing the reality of the social inequality of racialized persons in the United States. Rooting continuing social inequality in the fact that racialized persons have comparatively little social value highlights that in the contemporary age, their social equality is *simply not a priority*. What I like about Lebron's description of the continuing social inequality of racialized persons is that it captures the indirect and somewhat nonchalant (but no less oppressive) way racial oppression operates in the contemporary age. No, there are no more public lynchings, but this does not mean that the problems racialized persons face (and that were generated by hundreds of years of enforced, hereditary chattel servitude, and then perpetuated for decades thereafter in the form of Jim Crow laws and social morés and laws designed to humiliate and degrade) have disappeared. Where there were once lynchings, there remain systemic social attitudes and beliefs that continue to make the goal of human flourishing far more challenging for racialized persons than for nonracialized persons. If we can, as a society, acknowledge this reality, the first step will be taken toward providing much-needed social change en route to social equality.

In my view, Lebron well captures—to borrow a term from Hannah Arendt—the *banality* of how racial oppression and the perpetuation of racial inequality work in the contemporary United States (see Arendt 1963). Racial inequality in the United States today is business-as-usual, unworthy of comment, routine, and ordinary. It is a part of the contemporary age, an everyday phenomenon, like social media and rapid technological advancement. To a certain extent Lebron is saying that (mainstream/nonracialized) Americans are lazy and lacking in moral fiber or chops. They are fat cats sitting around in their material comfort, indifferent and oblivious to the tragic and often horrific circumstances in which a large percentage of their fellow citizens live. But, Lebron is more hopeful than I feel comfortable being about America's ability to pull itself up by its own bootstraps, put on its big person pants, and develop a backbone (a better "character") when it comes to these issues. Recent political events have reinforced my cynicism on this topic.[9] So, while Lebron is able to be optimistic about the possibility of America's reshaping its "character" spontaneously and *on its own* (i.e., motivated purely by revelations—and subsequent ameliorative actions—that might come from having some sort of moral epiphany about the inappropriateness of its apathy on the topic of racial equality), as of the time of the writing of this book, I am not as able to be optimistic. However, I am doing what I believe I can do to try to address the problem of the continuing inequality of racialized persons in the United States, and that is use my legal and philosophical education and training to recommend changes in the laws.

CRITICAL RACE THEORY

Critical Race Theory is a branch of jurisprudence that self-consciously takes account of the experiences of racialized persons in its assessment of the meaning and appropriate application of laws. It is suspicious of liberal legal theory's ability to grapple with the continuing unequal status of racialized persons in the United States.

Origins: The Work of Derrick Bell

Critical Race Theory begins with the scholarship of Harvard law professor, Derrick Bell. In 1973, Bell famously broke new ground in jurisprudence with the publication of the first casebook on the intersection of race, racism, and American law (see Bell 1973). "[T]his book," wrote Bell plainly, at the top of the preface of the book, "is concerned with American racism initiated by whites against blacks, and seeks to determine to what extent that racism is reflected in the law" (Bell 1973, xxxix). In that book, and in subsequent scholarship, Bell searches the history of the relationship between law and racialized persons in the United States for information on the extent to which racism was responsible for the rather haphazard application of certain principles thought to be inherent in the American ethos (such as liberty, equality, freedom, autonomy, "natural rights," "fundamental rights," and the so-called pursuit of happiness) to legal disputes involving racialized persons (See, e.g., Bell 1976; Bell 1980; Bell 1992a; Bell 1992b, Bell 2004).

In his search for information, Bell's inquiry often begins with the 1954 decision in *Brown v. Board of Education*, the landmark civil rights case that (at least ostensibly) overruled *Plessy v. Ferguson* on the topic of whether "separate" public facilities and accommodations meant "equal" facilities for the purposes of meeting the requirements of the Equal Protection Clause of the Fourteenth Amendment. While the Court had held in *Plessy* that separate public facilities for racialized and nonracialized persons satisfied the requirements of the Equal Protection Clause as long as both public facilities were "equal," the *Brown* Court held that when it came to public schools (and by implication any public facilities), "separate" meant *inherently* unequal, such that separate public schools for racialized and nonracialized persons were facially unconstitutional. With the decision in *Brown,* in other words, the Court outlawed racially segregated schools across the United States, simultaneously outlawing racially segregated public facilities of all kinds in the process.

For Bell, however, and many others, the decision in *Brown* was a bit of a conundrum in the history of the relationship between race, racism, and American law. This is because, despite popular views to the contrary, the demand by racialized persons for equal access to public education was not a new phenomenon in American life in 1954, the year *Brown* was decided, quite the contrary. Racialized persons in the United States had been demanding equal access to public education for approximately one hundred years before *Brown* to no avail. Up to the decision in *Brown,* the demand for equal access to public education on the part of racialized persons in the United States had always been met with orders that separate schools be made equal. *Brown* suddenly changed all of that, and Bell was curious as to why.

He found a possible explanation for the sudden change in policy in evidence that the *Brown* decision had *operated in the interests of nonracialized persons overall.* In a provocative essay published in the *Harvard Law Review,* Bell cites certain economic and political advances both "at home and abroad" that followed from the abandonment of racial segregation in the United States (Bell 1980, 524). "First, the decision helped to provide immediate credibility to America's struggle with Communist countries to win the hearts and minds of third world peoples" (ibid.). "Second, *Brown* offered much needed reassurance to American blacks that the precepts of equality and freedom so heralded during World War II might yet be given meaning at home" (Bell 1980, 524–25). "Finally," suggests Bell, "there were whites who realized that the South could make the transition from a rural, plantation society to the sunbelt with all its potential and profit only when it ended its struggle to remain divided by state-sponsored segregation. Thus, segregation was viewed as a barrier to further industrialization in the South," and desegregation removed that barrier (Bell 1980, 525).

On the basis of these observations, Bell suggests that just as slavery very likely would not have been abolished in the United States if the only motivating factor were the goal of racial equality, similarly racial segregation very likely would not have been abolished (in *Brown*) if the only motivating factor were racial equality. Instead, in both cases, it was the convergence of interests of racialized persons (racial equality) and the interests of nonracialized persons (economic, political, etc.) that accounted for the result. The phenomenon of the interests of racialized and nonracialized persons combining together to explain (anomalous) progress in racial equality Bell called the principle of "interest convergence" (Bell 1980, 523). According to the principle of interest convergence, progress toward racial equality occurs in the United States, but only when accompanied by some clear advantage (usually an economic advantage) to the interests of nonracialized persons.

The move Bell makes here is arguably Marxian. Marxist legal theory is inquiry into the relationship between law and the reproduction of structural inequalities that characterize capitalist societies (Hunt 1999). The key idea in Marxist legal theory is that law is a specific form of social relation. It is a social relation between "legal subjects." The "legal subject" does not coincide with the natural person, however. Instead, the "legal subject" is an entity recognized by the legal system as a bearer of rights. Law as a specific type of social relation always generates what Karl Marx called a potential "mode of regulation." The discourse on rights, for example, should be understood as a mode of regulation between the attribution of rights and various legal subjects located within social relations. The discourse of rights provides a backdrop within which social relations can be made subject to a common discursive apparatus. This apparatus is internally inconsistent, however, and contains contradictions that highlight problems with the mode of regulation itself. These problems lead to instances of the failure of the law to adequately protect legitimate interests and claims. A central theme of Marxist legal theory (a theme that is ignored inside of traditional "rights based" legal theory) is that law manifests the interests of the dominant class. A related theme is that law is ideological in nature, both exemplifying and legitimating the values of the dominant class. Both of these themes originate in the early writings of Marx and Friedrich Engels (see Marx 1843/1994, Marx 1859/1994, Marx 1967, Marx and Engels 1846/1994).

Although law is identified by Marx and Engels as an integral part of the ideology of any society, Marx and Engels never developed a formal theory of law qua theory of law based on these ideas. The first full development of a Marxist theory of law came later, in 1929, from Evgeny Pashukanis, who articulated what is known as the commodity exchange theory of law (Pashukanis 2017). According to this theory, economics are central to the organization of society, and the legal and moral principles and institutions of society constitute what Marx and Engels called a "superstructure" that reflects the society's economics. On this view, law (all law) is inextricably linked to capitalism and hopelessly bourgeois. For Pashukanis, law itself would be unnecessary outside of capitalism since law's only use is as a way to mediate conflicting property interest inside of capitalist society. By contrast, in a socialist society, what would take the place of law and so-called individual rights would be a sort of quasi-utilitarianism which values collective satisfaction over the perceived need to protect the individual interests of individual legal subjects.

Arguably, Derrick Bell's principle of interest convergence—or the idea that legal advancements that operate in the interest of racial equality can only be achieved if they are accompanied by the furtherance of the (usually economic) interests of the dominant class, i.e., nonracialized persons—flows somewhat directly from a Marxist theory of law, particularly as envisioned by Pashukanis. On this view, there are no rights other than those that mediate economic disputes between individuals of the dominant or ruling class. Where there are no rights, there are no duties to respect those rights, no duties on the part of the ruling, nonracialized elite to respect the "rights" (to equality or anything else) of anyone, except to the extent that the economic interests of nonracialized persons are also advanced. Law works not to protect the powerless, but to keep the powerless in check so that the powerful can pursue and advance their own ends. Laws on this view are forces of oppression rather than emancipation, chains rather than instruments of liberation, particularly for the poor or otherwise marginalized or alienated from the ruling elite class. Charles Mills has recognized the connection many see (including himself) between Marxism and Critical Race Theory (see, e.g., Mills 2009). For Mills, a Marxist account of Critical Race Theory is "one that locates the emergence of race and white supremacy in the history of European imperialism, in bourgeois class interests and projects, while also recognizing that—*once created*—race achieves a certain autonomy of its own which requires the rethinking of orthodox white Marxisms" (ibid., 272).

In 2004, Bell followed up on his interest convergence theory of progress in the area of racial equality with a list of three "interest convergence covenants" that predate the decision in *Brown* and provide further evidence for his theory that "relief from racial discrimination has come only when policymakers recognize that such relief will provide a clear benefit for the nation or portions of the populace" (Bell 2004, 49). These three "covenants" are (1) the abolition of slavery in the northern states, (2) the Emancipation Proclamation, and (3) the Civil War amendments to the U.S. Constitution.

The abolition of slavery in the northern states, according to Bell, was met with resistance when the question of who would compensate the slave owner for the loss of property if abolition was enacted came up. In Pennsylvania, Rhode Island, Connecticut, New York, and New Jersey, according to Bell, gradual (rather than immediate) abolition statutes were enacted that were designed to lessen the financial burden that abolition would place on the slave owner. Under these gradual abolition statutes, "slaves were forced to pay, through their labor, almost 100 percent of their market value during long years as 'indentured servants'" (ibid., 51). Most importantly, it was clear that the northern states did not intend the abolition of slavery to be equated with the social acceptance of racialized persons. Bell cites Leon Litwack as observing, "Until the post–Civil War era, in fact, most northern whites would maintain a careful distinction between granting [racialized persons] legal protection—a *theoretical* right to life, liberty, and property—and political and social equality" (ibid., 52; emphasis added).

Perhaps an even more interesting case of a Bellian "interest convergence covenant" is the Emancipation Proclamation. Although, according to Bell, "adequate evidence shows that [President] Lincoln hated slavery," (ibid., 52), in his first inaugural speech, Lincoln denied any inclination to interfere with the institution in the states where it existed. Moreover, the prevailing view in the North was that the Civil War was intended to save the union, not to end slavery. Lincoln's own writings confirm that preserving the union was his primary goal. In a letter to abolitionist Horace Greeley, Lincoln stated, among other things, "If I could save the Union without freeing all the slaves, I would do it; and if I could save the Union without freeing any slave, I would do it; and if I could save it by freeing some and leaving others alone, I would also do that. *What I do about slavery and the colored race, I do because I believe it helps to save the Union*" (ibid., 53; emphasis added). According to Bell, at a time when the North needed troops, Lincoln, aware that a document claiming to end slavery would allow the enlistment of thousands of racialized persons in the Union army, told a group of people pleading for emancipation, "I view the matter as a practical war measure to be decided upon according to the advantages or disadvantages it may offer to the suppression of the rebellion" (ibid., 54). Pointedly, the Emancipation Proclamation actually *freed no slaves,* since it was limited to those areas still under Confederate control. Its effects were more symbolic than substantive, such that it is difficult to say with confidence that the Emancipation Proclamation actually helped racialized persons in any way.

Finally, Bell cites the Civil War Amendments as an example of interest convergence at work. According to Bell, the Amendments were enacted more to ensure Republican control of Congress and to prevent southerners from reasserting the political power they had exercised during the Civil War than as specific protection for the rights of racialized persons.

The legal scholarship of Derrick Bell, then, opened up the questions with which critical race theorists are still grappling today, and that form the backdrop of this book. Bell asked in the mid-1970s, and then throughout his long career, what role American race and racism played in the history and development of American jurisprudence and/or in the efforts toward progress on the topic of racial equality. His answer, surprisingly, was not that big a role. Instead, to the extent that progress in service of racial equality has been made in American society, it has not been motivated by a focus on race or by any attempt to eradicate American racism. Instead, small, incremental steps toward racial equality have been made almost *inadvertently*, as a consequence of coinciding with the achievement of some other, larger, more widely applicable objective that furthered the interests of the nonracialized.

Critical Race Theory and Equality

An interrogation into the meaning of equality in American jurisprudence has been a common focal point of Critical Race Theory in the years since Bell first began his important work in this area. For example, Linda S. Greene has expressed concern as to whether meaningful equality can be obtained for racialized persons through law (Greene 1990, 1517). After reviewing a series of Supreme Court cases decided in 1989 that all had the effect of limiting the scope of redress for the continued inequalities plaguing racialized persons, Greene found several disturbing themes in proto-twenty-first-century equality law. Citing "formalistic and hypertechnical reasoning" as at least one cause of these outcomes, Greene carefully examines several of the cases and finds several themes. The themes include: (1) the tendency to reduce all questions of racial equality to political questions, thereby stripping constitutional legitimacy from racial civil rights, and (2) the tendency to give legal legitimacy to the efforts of nonracialized persons, who historically have benefitted from racism, to maintain the racial status quo (ibid.).

On the reduction of questions of racial equality to political questions, Greene cites, for example, Justice O'Connor's words in *City of Richmond v. J.A. Croson Co.*, in which the Justice differentiates between "identified discrimination" and "societal discrimination" in order to conclude that the minority set aside program at issue in *Croson* was not adopted to remedy "identified discrimination" (which could only be shown through prima facie proof that the absence of minority contractors was due to constitutional or statutory violations) but (mere) social discrimination. This despite evidence that Richmond's population was 50 percent racialized persons and only 0.67 percent of the city's prime construction contracts had gone to racialized persons, plus evidence showing that many contractors' associations had no racialized persons among their members.

On the tendency to give legal legitimacy to the efforts of the nonracialized, who historically have benefitted from racism, Greene cites, among other cases, *Wards Cove Packing Co. v. Antonio*, in which an employer's policies that perpetuated segregation in employment were upheld as neutral, although the record revealed that the employer hired—"season after season"—predominantly nonracialized workers in its skilled positions and predominantly racialized persons (Alaskan natives) in its unskilled positions, and the fact that the employer maintained racially segregated housing and dining facilities. For Greene, this case prioritized the rights of nonracialized persons by offering legitimacy to segregated job categories, thereby benefitting the historical beneficiaries of segregation, and simultaneously granting legal immunity to employers using such categories by "stacking the litigation deck in their favor" (Greene 1990, 1533).

Addressing the problem of unconscious racism and its role in the perpetuation of racial inequality is a key theme in Critical Race Theory. Charles R. Lawrence III has written of the problem of unconscious racism in "The Id, The Ego, and Equal Protection: Reckoning with Unconscious Racism" (Lawrence 1995). There, Lawrence addresses the familiar problem in equal protection law of the difference the Supreme Court has traditionally seen between laws or policies that have "discriminatory intent" and laws or policies that have (mere) "disparate impact." Within liberal legal theory, discriminatory intent is unconstitutional but disparate impact is not. For Lawrence, this distinction is very odd indeed given that much harmful racial discrimination happens unconsciously, or even with *good* intentions. Much racism happens unconsciously, for Lawrence, *not* because the discriminatory actions in question are not motivated by racism (against racialized persons), but more often because persons engaging in such racism (usually liberals) *are not aware that their actions are motivated by racism,* and, in some sense, *cannot* come to grips with the possibility that their actions are motivated by racism, because to do so would strain their self-conceptions.

But, Lawrence has a solution: "Understanding unconscious motivation will . . . help us comprehend and combat the hegemony of the ideology of equal opportunity. A considerable body of scholarship from the academic left has analyzed the law as a hegemonic tool of domination. According to one theory, domination occurs when the ruling class gains the consent of the dominated classes through a system of ideas that reinforces the morality or the inevitability *of the existing order*. This 'interest theory' sees ideology as a consciously wielded weapon, an intellectual tool that a group uses to enhance its political power by *institutionalizing a particular view of reality*" (Lawrence 1995, 239; emphasis added). Moreover, according to another theory that draws upon theories of unconscious motivation, "ideology is a defense mechanism against the anxiety felt by those who hold power through means and with motives *they cannot comfortably acknowledge.* This 'strain theory' explains ideology as a response to the strains that an individual's or a group's social role or position creates. . . . Ideology enables privileged individuals to continue practices they would otherwise condemn and in which their own complicity would be painful to admit" (ibid.). For Lawrence, this understanding of ideology provides key information into society's (and the Supreme Court's) resistance to abandoning "one of its most critical conceptual images: the intent requirement" (ibid.). Those resistant to abandoning the intent requirement often claim that without it, there is no way to effectively measure that (unconscious) racist beliefs motivated behaviors or policies that have a disparate impact on racialized persons.

To meet this concern, Lawrence suggests what he calls the "cultural meaning test" according to which if plaintiffs produce enough evidence that a substantial number of people would blame disparate impact on the victims of the disparate impact themselves, particularly on essentialist grounds (e.g., all of the racialized persons and none of the nonracialized persons failed the written test conferring promotion not because the test was culturally skewed but because racialized persons are just less intelligent), *then racist motivations for the action can be reasonably attributed to the perpetrators of the action,* resulting in an equal protection violation. As Lawrence puts it, "[Plaintiffs] would seek to convince the court that most people in our culture believe that the average white person is inherently smarter than the average black person and that whites will interpret the racially selective impact of the test as a confirmation of that belief" (ibid., 253). However, Lawrence emphasizes that the greatest stumbling block to any attempt to quantify disparate impact in such a way as to acknowledge unconscious racism (and therefore find equal protection violations where laws or policies disparately impact racialized persons), is not logistics or proof, but "the perception among those who give substance to our jurisprudence *that it will operate against their self-interest*" (ibid., 255; emphasis added). While it is true, for Lawrence, that racism continues to be "aided and abetted" by "self-conscious bigots," the reality is that racism is just as much aided and abetted by well-meaning liberals, and operates as an "unconscious defense mechanism against the guilt and anxiety of those who hold power and privilege through means and with motives that they cannot [and will not] acknowledge" (ibid.). Certainly, the suggestion in this book is that the contemporary interpretation of the Equal Protection Clause can be understood to involve unconscious racism, of a kind imbedded in the concepts of biological race and legal equality.

In other words, it is not my claim that the Justices of the Supreme Court are card-carrying (that is, conscious) racists who utilize biological race and legal equality to inform their interpretation of the Equal Protection Clause in such a way as to deliberately alienate and harm (exclude from equal protection) racialized persons for the benefit of nonracialized persons. Instead, my claim is that the choices the Court has been making in recent equal protection cases evidence the same sort of unconscious (but nonetheless damaging) racism of which Charles Lawrence speaks.

NOTES

1. The description of legal hermeneutics outlined in this section is largely taken from Botts 2014.

2. Intentionalist interpretive methods are those in which the so-called "intent of the Framers" is sought and considered the ultimate authority on what the constitution means.

3. What I am calling "non-originalism" is also known by the less neutral term of "judicial activism," a pejorative term used by those whose approach to constitutional meaning leans more toward originalism.

4. This approach has recently been called "textualism" by Supreme Court Justice Antonin Scalia and others (Scalia 1997).

5. The reader should note that the divide between originalism and non-originalism is akin to the divide between epistemological foundationalism and antifoundationalism.

6. It should be noted that the legal hermeneutical approach to constitutional interpretation overlaps in important ways with what Philip Bobbit has called the six "modalities" of constitutional interpretation: (1) history, (2) text, (3) structure, (4) doctrine, (5) ethos, and (6) prudence (Bobbit 1996, 1999: 126). There is also overlap between the legal hermeneutical anti-method and the following approaches to meaning in the law: Dennis Patterson's postmodern account (Patterson 1996/1999), Paul Campos's approach (Campos 1992), and the approach of legal pragmatism (see, e.g., Richard Warner's approach; Warner 1996/1999).

7. See also Hoy 1987 and Hoy 1985.

8. McGary is careful to point out that neither the integrationists nor the separatists are demographically or ideologically monolithic, and that he is using these terms to capture a divide amongst racialized persons that, while inexact, is helpful in terms of understanding conflicting approaches to the problem of the continuing problems faced by racialized persons.

9. At the time of this writing, Donald J. Trump has been president of the United States for just over half a year. Over the past weekend, there was a riot in Charlottesville, Virginia, in which white supremacist and "alt-right" groups marched through the streets carrying confederate flags and guns, one of them running an automobile into a crowd of people at a certain point, killing at least one person. More white supremacist rallies are scheduled for next weekend.

TWO

Equal Protection and Racialized Persons

The Equal Protection Clause of the Fourteenth Amendment to the United States Constitution states: "No State shall make or enforce any law which shall . . . deny to any person within its jurisdiction equal protection of the laws." But, while the equal protection law that developed in the wake of the adoption of the Fourteenth Amendment was meant to protect racialized persons from the unequal treatment under the law they faced after the end of slavery and the end of the Civil War, equal protection law currently fails to do this. Instead, the most recent cases brought under the Equal Protection Clause have protected nonracialized persons from racial discrimination more so than racialized persons.

The very first cases to interpret the Fourteenth Amendment after its ratification held that the purpose of the Equal Protection Clause was to protect former slaves. These were a conglomeration of cases decided in 1873 known as *The Slaughterhouse Cases*. In 1869, the Louisiana legislature had enacted a statute that gave a monopoly for the city of New Orleans to a slaughterhouse. Several nonracialized butchers filed suit in state courts seeking injunctions against the monopoly. The butchers were unable to obtain the injunctions in state courts so they turned to the U.S. Supreme Court. Among other things, they claimed that the Louisiana law denied them equal protection of the laws. The Supreme Court held that the butchers had not been denied equal protection of the laws. The Fourteenth Amendment, it held, was intended to protect former slaves only and could not be broadly applied.

The very next case to decide the meaning of the Fourteenth Amendment, the 1880 case of *Strauder v. West Virginia,* also held that the Equal Protection Clause was designed as a protection for former slaves. The Equal Protection Clause, the Court stated, was there to protect what it called "the colored race" from legal discrimination against them on the basis of their status as colored persons. Strauder was a racialized man who had been convicted of murder by a jury composed entirely of nonracialized persons. The law of the State of West Virginia at the time precluded racialized persons from serving on juries.[1] Strauder's contention was that the West Virginia law violated his rights under the Equal Protection Clause. The Supreme Court agreed. The Fourteenth Amendment, the Court said, was intended to secure to the recently emancipated race all of the civil rights enjoyed by others and confers a positive immunity or right to exemption from legislation directed against them as colored persons. This immunity, the Court said, implied an exemption for racialized persons from all discrimination which implied legal inferiority, which lessened the security of their rights, or which amounted to an attempt to reduce them to a condition of a subject race. The West Virginia law in question violated the Equal Protection Clause, said the Court, because it discriminated against racialized persons in these ways.

THE RISE OF SEPARATE BUT EQUAL DOCTRINE

But, just three years later in 1883, with the decision in *The Civil Rights Cases,* the Court began to distinguish between racial discrimination on the part of the government ("public" discrimination) and racial discrimination by private citizens ("private" racial discrimination), and this distinction became one of the bases upon which legalized racial discrimination in places of public accommodation was established a few years later, in the case of *Plessy v. Ferguson,* discussed below. The issue in *The Civil Rights Cases* was the constitutionality of a section of the Civil Rights Act of 1875 which criminalized even private discrimination on the basis of any "previous condition of servitude" in places of public accommodation. The Supreme Court said that this section of the Civil Rights Act was unconstitutional because the Fourteenth Amendment was a prohibition against government ("state") action only, not acts by private citizens, such that a federal law that criminalized private racial discrimination could not be sustained.[2] In effect, the Supreme Court was claiming that private discrimination against racialized persons did not violate the Equal Protection Clause and was not unconstitutional. Much would be made of this public/private distinction as the question of the constitutional rights of racialized persons in public accommodations and public schools became an increasingly pressing one in the twentieth century.

The distinction the Court made in *The Civil Rights Cases* between public and private racial discrimination was made again in the landmark case of *Plessy v. Ferguson,* decided in 1896. As mentioned above, this distinction formed the basis of what became known as Separate But Equal Doctrine emerging from *Plessy,* or the view that the dictates of the Equal

Protection Clause could be satisfied by providing "equal" accommodations for racialized persons and for nonracialized persons, even if those accommodations were kept "separate."

At issue in *Plessy* was a Louisiana law known as the Separate Car Act which required "equal, but separate" railway car accommodations for racialized and nonracialized persons. Violation of this law was a misdemeanor. Homer Plessy, a racialized man of mixed racial ancestry, deliberately violated the law by sitting in a railway car designated for nonracialized persons only and was convicted of the misdemeanor.[3] He appealed to the Louisiana Supreme Court, who upheld the Louisiana law. Plessy appealed to the U.S. Supreme Court. The Court agreed with the state supreme court and upheld the Louisiana law. Citing, among other things, *The Civil Rights Cases*, the Court reasoned that the owner of a public conveyance cannot be regarded as imposing any badge of slavery or servitude; and for this reason, there was no equal protection violation in the Louisiana law. While the Fourteenth Amendment was designed to abolish *legal* distinctions between racialized persons and nonracialized persons, the Court reasoned, the Amendment certainly could not have been designed to abolish *social* distinctions. In the twentieth century, however, this legal/social (a.k.a. public/private) distinction would come to be challenged as a pretense for attempts on the part of the government to perpetuate the unequal status of racialized persons after the Civil War.[4]

In addition, where public accommodations for "coloreds" were "equal" to the accommodations provided for nonracialized persons, the Court in *Plessy* stated, there was *no equal protection violation*, since the mere fact of social separation did not impose any badge of slavery. Inherent in this conclusion are at least three subconclusions. First, taking the lead from *The Civil Rights Cases*, the owner of a public conveyance is not a state actor, not acting on behalf of the government, and only a state actor can impose the badges of slavery. Second, even if the owner of a public conveyance were a state actor, and could impose the badges of slavery, a constitutionally significant bright line can be drawn between "legal" racial distinctions and "social" ones. Third, the owner of a private business is constitutionally at liberty to make "social" racial distinctions.

The Separate But Equal Doctrine officially created by *Plessy v. Ferguson* had a long reign. The doctrine was in place from 1896 to 1954 and had many distinctive features, chief among them the making of an official legal distinction between nonracialized and racialized Americans on the federal level by the Supreme Court of the United States. Although what are known as Jim Crow laws or Black Codes had been appearing in state statutory systems all over the south ever since the Emancipation Proclamation of 1862,[5] *Plessy* provided federal sanction for those laws and paved the way for more rigorous enactment and enforcement of them (Tribe 1988; Stephens & Scheb 2008). Segregation in public accommodations such as trains, buses, hotels, swimming pools, and other places of public amusement became a way of life all over America, a legal and social fact that became a part of the fabric and identity of the American culture. Some recent scholarship has called this phenomenon the development in America of a "racial consciousness" that has become a permanent feature of American life (Bell 1992b; Banton 1988; Lawson 2008; Feagin 2006).[6] These scholars argue that the idea that racialized persons and nonracialized persons could or should be socially segregated on the basis of race became regarded by many Americans, particularly subconsciously, as a self-evident truth.

Separate But Equal Doctrine, then, was an early method of interpreting the Equal Protection Clause that was established by the landmark case of *Plessy v. Ferguson* in 1896. Distinctive features of Separate But Equal Doctrine were (1) that it incorporated into the official Supreme Court interpretation of the meaning of the Equal Protection Clause an explicit, federal endorsement of a legal differentiation between racialized and nonracialized Americans, (2) that it made a constitutionally significant distinction between "legal" racial discrimination and "social" racial discrimination, with "social" racial discrimination considered constitutionally permissible, (3) that distinction between nonracialized persons and racialized persons on the part of the owner of public conveyances or other places of public accommodation was considered a "social" distinction rather than a "legal" one, and that (4) the ideal of equality contemplated by the Equal Protection Clause was thought to be achieved in public accommodations if "separate but equal" facilities were provided for each of "the two races."

WHAT IS EQUAL PROTECTION?

In 1938, the court began to reconsider Separate But Equal Doctrine. In the case of *Missouri ex rel. Gaines v. Canada*, petitioner Lloyd Gaines, a racialized man, was denied admission to the law school at the University of Missouri. The state of Missouri admitted that Gaines was qualified—in terms of his previous work and college credits—to be admitted into the law school, but asserted that it was contrary to the constitution, laws, and public policy of the State to admit a racialized person as a student at the University of Missouri. There was provision made in the state statutes, however, for funding to be provided for racialized students to attend law schools out of state rather than attend law school at the University of Missouri. Gaines considered the state's action in this case to be an equal protection violation and appealed the decision to the Supreme Court. The Court concluded that because the state of Missouri did not provide a separate but equal law school for racialized students, the decision of the state court not to admit Gaines had to be overturned. In *Gaines*, then, while the Supreme Court acknowledged the difficulties of providing separate but equal facilities for every racialized student, at the same time the Court began to highlight the question of just what "equal" meant in equal protection law.[7]

RACIAL DISCRIMINATION PER SE BEGINS: JAPANESE AMERICANS AFTER WWII

Then in 1944, the Court decided *Korematsu v. United States.* In that case, Korematsu, an American citizen of Japanese descent, was convicted in a federal district court of remaining in San Leandro, California, contrary to a law which directed that, after May 9, 1942, all persons of Japanese ancestry should be excluded from that area. Korematsu appealed to the Supreme Court contending that the order violated his rights under the Equal Protection Clause. Although the Court concluded that the order did *not* violate Korematsu's right to equal protection under the Fourteenth Amendment, it also held that *all legal restrictions which curtail the civil rights of a single racial group are immediately suspect* and should be subjected to "the most rigid scrutiny." In other words, the *Korematsu* Court suggested that the Equal Protection Clause should be understood or interpreted to provide special protection for a racial group when a given law negatively implicates the rights of that group qua group. With the *Korematsu* case, the Court began to find legalized racial discrimination *per se* problematic rather than racial discrimination against racialized persons.

SOCIAL SEGREGATION

Six years later in *McLaurin v. Oklahoma State Regents* (1950), the Court began to rethink its position that public and private discrimination were legally separable issues. In *McLaurin,* officials at the University of Oklahoma had attempted to segregate a racialized graduate student seeking a doctorate in education at the University of Oklahoma from his nonracialized colleagues after he was admitted by a court order. In class, the student was required to sit in a row of desks restricted to racialized persons. He was required to eat at a designated table in the cafeteria and was even prohibited from visiting his professors during their regular office hours in order to minimize his interactions with nonracialized students. The Court held that these restrictions significantly detracted from the student's educational experience and thus could not be justified. Instead, once the student was admitted to the school, the school had an obligation to treat McLaurin the same as the other students, as this was the only way the constitutional requirement that he receive an "equal" education could be accomplished. Significant here is that the segregation to which McLaurin was subjected was largely *social,* and that the Court found in this case a relationship between the constitutional requirement of *legal* equality and the social segregation and discrimination to which McLaurin was subject.

Separate as Inferior

Then, in *Sweatt v. Painter* (1950), the Court had an opportunity to assess the constitutionality of an attempt by the state of Texas to provide a "separate but equal" law school for a lone racialized student. Petitioner Sweatt had been refused admission to the University of Texas law school solely because he was a racialized person. The University of Texas law school was restricted to nonracialized students in accordance with state law.[8] Nonracialized law students went to the University of Texas, but racialized ones were to be sent to the Texas College for Negroes. The Court found that the law school for racialized persons was substantially inferior, in terms of both measurable and intangible factors, to the law school that only admitted nonracialized persons, and held that the Fourteenth Amendment therefore required the University of Texas to admit Sweatt to the University of Texas law school. After *Sweatt,* it seemed unlikely that the Supreme Court would continue to employ Separate But Equal doctrine in the realm of publically funded education since the educational services provided for racialized persons under that doctrine were in fact not "equal" but inferior. In the process, the line between legal and social equality became further blurred.

SEPARATE BUT EQUAL OVERTURNED

Then, in 1954, the court explicitly overturned Separate But Equal Doctrine in public education in the landmark case of *Brown v. Board of Education* (also known as *Brown I*). There, a unanimous Court held that separate educational facilities for racialized children were *inherently* unequal, and that there was no place in publically funded education for Separate But Equal Doctrine. The Court was unsure, however, as to how desegregation of public education should be accomplished and did not make its first decision on that issue until 1955 in a case known as *Brown II.* In *Brown II,* faced with widespread resistance, often violent, to its decision in *Brown I* in the South, the Court decided to leave the decision as to how to accomplish desegregation of public education to the federal district judges in the various states. The Court ordered that the states proceed with "all deliberate speed," a phrase that came to be associated with delaying tactics on the part of the Southern states (Stephens & Scheb 2008, 459). This decision resulted in the usage of various delaying tactics for the next ten years or so by state and local officials, particularly in the southern states, and the establishment of no clear guidelines regarding how to accomplish equal educational facilities for racialized children (ibid.). But, after *Brown I and II*, it was clear that the Court considered Separate But Equal Doctrine to be unconstitutional and ineffective at accomplishing the Fourteenth Amendment ideal of equality for racialized persons, at least in the realm of public education.

Then, in *Alexander v. Holmes County Board of Education* (1969), the Court stated that desegregation of public schools should occur "at once," signaling that it would no longer tolerate the South's delaying tactics (ibid.).

RACIAL CLASSIFICATIONS AND MARRIAGE

The question of legalized racial discrimination deployed to achieve social ends took center stage in a dispute over the constitutionality of anti-miscegenation laws in the 1967 case of *Loving v. Virginia.* In that case, Mildred Jeter, a racialized woman, and Richard Loving, a nonracialized man—both residents of Virginia—were legally married in the District of Columbia in 1958. Shortly after their marriage, the Lovings returned home to Virginia where they were soon charged with the crime of violating Virginia's ban on interracial marriages. The Lovings pleaded guilty to the charge, and were sentenced to one year in jail. Their sentences were suspended on the condition that they leave Virginia and not return to the state together for twenty-five years. The Lovings appealed their convictions and sentences on the ground that Virginia's anti-miscegenation laws violated the Fourteenth Amendment. The state of Virginia responded that since the anti-miscegenation laws applied equally to nonracialized persons and racialized persons, there was no equal protection violation. The Supreme Court disagreed. The court stated that criminal penalties for interracial marriage arose *as an incident to slavery,* and that the anti-miscegenation law in question was a development of Virginia's white supremacy laws,[9] the central feature of which was the absolute prohibition of a nonracialized person marrying anyone other than another nonracialized person. The Court held that there was patently no legitimate overriding purpose independent of invidious racial discrimination which justified the racial classification at issue in the case. The fact that Virginia prohibited only interracial marriages involving nonracialized persons, the Court said, demonstrated that the racial classifications were designed to maintain white supremacy. The implication of the Court's decision was that a law that is designed to maintain white supremacy is a law that violates equal protection and that where this is the case, invidious racial discrimination has occurred and the constitution has been violated.

The *Loving* case contains an unusually large amount of social analysis of the problem of racism in America. The Court wrote, for example, at page 6:

> Virginia is now one of 16 States which prohibit and punish marriages on the basis of racial classifications. Penalties for miscegenation arose as an incident to slavery, and have been common in Virginia since the colonial period. The present statutory scheme dates from the adoption of the Racial Integrity Act of 1924, passed during the period of extreme nativism which followed the end of the First World War. The central features of this Act, and current Virginia law, are the absolute prohibition of a "white person" marrying other than another "white person," a prohibition against issuing marriage licenses until the issuing official is satisfied that the applicants' statements as to their race are correct, certificates of "racial composition" to be kept by both local and state registrars, and the carrying forward of earlier prohibitions against racial intermarriage.

Notable about *Loving* is that while its holding is that racial classifications in marriage laws violate the Equal Protection Clause, the Supreme Court's explanation for why the particular racial classification at issue in *Loving* is unconstitutional is *the history of racial discrimination against racialized persons in Virginia*. Virginia's antimiscegenation law *could not be benign*, the Court argued, because the social context indicated that antimiscegenation laws in Virginia had always been designed to perpetuate white supremacy, and *not because* racial classifications *per se* were constitutionally problematic. In *Loving*, then, the Court is still identifying racial discrimination *against racialized persons* as the problem to be solved by equal protection law, rather than racial discrimination *per se*.

DISCRIMINATORY INTENT VS. DISCRIMINATORY IMPACT

The case of *Washington v. Davis* (1976) added the new concept of "disparate impact" to equal protection law. In this case, Harley and Sellers, two racialized men whose applications to become police officers in Washington, DC, were rejected, filed suit against the District of Columbia claiming that the DC Police Department's recruiting procedures, which included a written personnel test known as "Test 21," were racially discriminatory in violation of the constitution.[10] The police department claimed that the test was designed to test verbal ability, vocabulary, reading and comprehension. Harley and Seller claimed that the test bore no relationship to job performance, excluded a disproportionately high number of "Negro" applicants, and for these reasons was unconstitutional. The Court upheld Test 21. The test was *racially neutral on its face*, said the Court, and since no one, not even Harley or Sellers, was claiming that the test involved a racially discriminatory *intent*, it was constitutional.

The fact that the test had, or may have had, a discriminatory *impact* was inapposite, said the Court. The test for the constitutionality of a law charged with being racially discriminatory in violation of the constitution was whether the law involved a racially discriminatory intent. The Court concluded that a law or policy having *merely a disparate impact* will be upheld unless plaintiffs can show that it was adopted to serve a racially discriminatory purpose. *Washington v. Davis*, then, adds to equal protection law the idea that where discriminatory *intent* cannot be demonstrated, racially discriminatory laws (against racialized persons) will be upheld.

But, the problem with this approach to equal protection law, as Kenji Yoshino points out, is that it "gets it exactly backward," ignoring the fact that the history of legalized racial discrimination in America is a history of dressing racism up in racially neutral clothes (Yoshino 2011, 767).[11] Using this distinction between discriminatory intent and disparate impact, the Court has over the years shifted from providing redress to racialized persons for laws that on the surface appear race-neutral but in practice operate to disenfranchise racialized persons, to not providing equal protection of the law to racialized persons at all unless the law in question is on its face discriminatory against racialized persons. This has had a dramatic chilling effect on the historical protection provided for racialized persons under the Equal Protection Clause (Yoshino 2011, 767). *Washington v. Davis* set the stage for the decision in the most damaging equal protection case to the equality rights of racialized persons: *Regents of the University of California v. Bakke* (1978), discussed next.

BAKKE: RACIAL DISCRIMINATION PER SE IS FORMALIZED

In *Regents of the University of California v. Bakke* (1978), the policy found to have violated equal protection of the law was actually designed *to help* racialized persons. In *Bakke*, a thirty-seven-year-old nonracialized male who was twice denied admission to the University of California at Davis medical school challenged the school's race-conscious policy, claiming that the policy violated his right to equal protection under the Fourteenth Amendment. The Supreme Court agreed, holding that laws involving racial classifications were subject to strict judicial scrutiny across the board and without regard to whether the group discriminated against by the law or policy was in the numerical minority or had suffered a history of political disenfranchisement. With *Bakke*, then, "reverse racism" was born, and received endorsement by the Supreme Court.

The details of *Bakke* are important. The race-conscious policy at issue involved what has come to be known as a "quota system." The Cal-Davis medical school had two tracks for admission: the "regular" track and the "special" track. The regular track required automatic rejection of anyone with a grade point average below 2.5. Then, about one out of six of those remaining were interviewed. After the interview, each candidate was rated on a scale of 1 to 100 by each of the admission committee members. This rating was known as a candidate's "benchmark score." The benchmark score was calculated in terms of the interviewers' summaries, the candidate's grade point average, the candidate's science course grade point average, the candidate's Medical College Admissions Test scores, letters of recommendation, extracurricular activities, and other biographical data. Based on the benchmark score, offers of admission were made. The committee also had a waiting list. The chair of the committee had the power to place people with "special skills" on the waiting list.

There were sixteen spaces available for "special" applicants. The special track was run by a separate committee comprised primarily of members of minority groups. The application forms at issue asked candidates whether they wished to be considered as "economically and/or educationally disadvantaged" applicants or members of a "minority group" (racialized persons, Chicanos, Asians, American Indians). If an applicant identified himself or herself to be "economically and/or educationally disadvantaged," he or she would be rated in a manner similar to the one employed by the general admissions committee. If a candidate identified himself or herself as a member of a "minority group" (racialized persons, Chicanos, Asians, and Native Americans), the candidate did not have to meet the 2.5 grade point cutoff. The special candidates were given benchmark scores and the top choices were given to the general admissions committee. The special committee continued to recommend candidates until sixteen special admission selections had been made.

Bakke was twice considered and rejected under the regular admissions program. In both years, special applicants were admitted with significantly lower scores than his. After his second rejection, Bakke filed suit in state court asking the court to compel his admission to the medical school, alleging that the special admissions program violated his rights under the Equal Protection Clause. The medical school cross-claimed for a declaration that its special admissions program was lawful. The Supreme Court invalidated the school's special admissions program on the ground that quota systems like the one used by the medical school operated so as to discriminate against applicants like Bakke, i.e., nonracialized applicants, on the basis of race in violation of the Fourteenth Amendment. The Court ordered Bakke's admission to the medical school.

After *Bakke* equal protection law has never been the same. While pre-*Bakke* equal protection law was there to protect racialized persons in virtue of the observable reality that the equality status of racialized persons was far below that of nonracialized persons in American society as a direct by-product of American chattel slavery, post-*Bakke* equal protection law is there to protect everyone from racial discrimination *per se*. The result is that nonracialized persons claiming equal protection violations are far more likely to succeed in court than racialized persons.

POST-*BAKKE* FALLOUT

From 1980 to 1989, the Court continued to utilize racial discrimination *per se* as the problem to be solved by equal protection law in a series of cases dealing with race-conscious policies and programs. There were cases in this period in which race-conscious programs were explicitly upheld,[12] cases where race-conscious policies and programs were limited in scope,[13] and cases of the explicit protection of nonracialized persons.[14] Then, in *City of Richmond v. J.A. Croson Company* (1989), the Court dealt a serious blow to race-conscious policies and programs when it struck down a Richmond set-aside plan requiring construction companies who were awarded city contracts to award at least 30 percent of their subcontracts to minority-owned businesses. The Court reasoned that the set-aside plan denied certain citizens—in this case nonracialized citizens—the opportunity to compete for a certain percentage of public contracts based solely on their race.

Then, in *Adarand Constructors, Inc. v. Peña* (1995), the Court affirmed its new view that racial discrimination *per se* was the problem to be solved by equal protection law. At issue in the case was a policy of the U.S. Department of Transportation under which general contractors were given a financial incentive to hire subcontractors run by individuals who were members of socially and economically disadvantaged groups. It was part of the policy that general contractors should presume that socially and economically disadvantaged individuals include racialized Americans, Hispanic Americans, Native Americans, Asian Pacific Americans, and other minorities. Although Adarand Constructors (which was owned and operated by nonracialized persons) submitted a lower bid, it was passed over as a subcontractor on a federal highway project in favor of a company that had preferred status under the race-conscious policy. The Court held that since the policy involved a racial classification, it violated equal protection of the laws (for nonracialized persons).

Gratz v. Bollinger and *Grutter v. Bollinger*, both decided in 2003 and together known as "the Michigan cases," represent the state of the law today on whether racial discrimination *per se* or racial discrimination against racialized persons is the problem to be addressed by equal protection law in cases of alleged racial discrimination.

At issue in *Gratz* was an undergraduate admissions policy used by the University of Michigan. According to the policy, each applicant was assigned a number of points based on several criteria including high school grades, strength of high school curriculum, standardized test scores, leadership, an essay, and membership in an underrepresented racial minority group. The total number of points available was 150 points. Twenty points were automatically awarded to any applicant who was a member of a racial minority group under the *Gratz* policy (the "designated points" policy).

At issue in *Grutter* was a law school admissions policy used by the University of Michigan Law School according to which all of the information in an applicant's file was reviewed by admissions officials individually. Each file included the applicant's undergraduate G.P.A., LSAT score, letters of recommendation, a personal statement, and an essay describing how the applicant would contribute to life at the law school, including a consideration of diversity under the *Grutter* policy (the "totality of the file" policy).

The designated points policy failed, but the totality of the file policy was upheld by the Supreme Court. The Court reasoned that automatic assignment of twenty points for being a member of a racial minority group was not a policy that was sufficiently "narrowly tailored" to meet the interest in educational diversity that the University claimed justified their program. The totality of the file policy, by contrast, was held constitutional (i.e., facilitated equal protection under the law, according to the Court) since it required consideration of each applicant on an individual basis and did not make an applicant's race the defining feature of his or her application.

CONCLUDING REFLECTIONS

Together *Gratz* and *Grutter* paint a portrait that is unfriendly to equal protection of the laws for racialized persons. Rather than acknowledging the great disadvantage experienced by racialized persons when applying to public professional schools and using equal protection law to take steps to ameliorate that damage, in adopting the totality of the file policy, the Court places racialized persons in the position of leaving their admission into public professional schools *completely at the discretion of the admission committees of those schools*. In holding that the totality of the file policy was more "narrowly tailored" to meet the university's interest in educational diversity than the designated points policy, the Court arguably appears to have denied that equal protection for racialized persons still requires the kind of proactive remedial intervention that the Equal Protection Clause was originally designed to effectuate.

Moreover, the Court's decision in *Grutter* (the "totality of the file" case) commits the original sin of Critical Race Theory, which is that it treats racial discrimination against racialized persons the same as racial discrimination against nonracialized persons. This picture of racial discrimination is in flagrant disregard of the systemic racialized discrimination that racialized persons continue to face in the United States as a direct legacy of the institution of chattel slavery of racialized persons that was legal from the country's inception until the Emancipation Proclamation of 1863 and the ratification of the Thirteenth Amendment to the U.S. Constitution in 1865.

Since *Grutter* is the defining and controlling Supreme Court decision in the area of equal protection law today (on the topic of racial discrimination), the state of affairs for equal protection of the laws for racialized persons is not good. According to the reasoning of this case, racialized persons are entitled to no more constitutional protection against racial discrimination than are nonracialized persons. As critical race theorists have been pointing out for the last twenty years or so, all laws purporting to universally apply to everyone (racialized and nonracialized alike) in a society such as American society in which there is pervasive and systemic inequality between racialized and nonracialized persons in every area of concern, universal and impartial application of the laws necessarily means the privileging of nonracialized interests over racialized interests. This is because universal application of laws to an unequal society does nothing other than preserve the (unequal) status quo.

But, as will be shown in chapter 3, the Supreme Court's switch from understanding racial discrimination as problematic because it perpetuates the "badges of slavery" for racialized persons to understanding racial discrimination as problematic *per se* (i.e., equally problematic for racialized persons and for nonracialized persons) can be shown to correlate with a switch on the Court's part, over time, from understanding the concept of race as culturally and historically derived to understanding the concept of race as biologically based. The switch can also be seen to correlate with a switch in focus on the part of the Supreme Court from social equality to legal equality, as will be shown in chapter 4. While the early equal protection cases speak of remedying the unequal status to which racialized persons were relegated owing to the institution of chattel slavery, more recent equal protection cases make no mention of this history or causal relationship. Instead, the concept of race is discussed as if it were an irrelevant, biological trait, on the basis of which it would simply be illogical to mete out access to social goods; and the urgent necessity felt by the drafters of the Equal Protection Clause to address the pervasive social inequality experienced by racialized persons after the end of the Civil War has all but disappeared from the Court's reasoning process. In the next chapter, the switch in the understanding of the concept of race on the part of the Supreme Court will be teased out in detail through philosophical analysis of the concept of race utilized in seminal and pivotal cases in the history of equal protection law.

NOTES

1. The West Virginia statute stated: "All white male persons who are twenty-one year of age and who are citizens of this State shall be liable to serve as jurors, except as herein provided" (Acts of 1872–1873, p. 102). The persons excepted were state officials.

2. The doctrine of state action is an integral part of equal protection analysis, but is not directly relevant to the issues that are the subject of the present inquiry. For further information on state action doctrine, see Tribe 1988 and Stephens and Scheb 2008.

3. I regularly refer to persons of mixed racialized and nonracialized ancestry as racialized persons, following the convention of racial categorization in the United States, rooted in the infamous "one drop rule," according to which any African heritage at all, even "one drop," rendered someone racialized. There is more on the "one drop rule" in chapter 3. Of course, there are other reasonable and legitimate ways of referring to persons of mixed racialized and nonracialized ancestry.

4. See, for example, *Brown v. Board of Education,* 347 U.S. 483 (1954).

5. Jim Crow laws or Black Codes were bodies of legislation enacted after the Civil War by the southern states to maintain the socially and legally inferior position of former slaves after the abolition of slavery (Du Bois 1935; Kull 1992; Woodward 1974/2006).

6. Ronald Dworkin has written, for example, that "American society is . . . a racially conscious society; this is the inevitable and evident consequence of a history of slavery, repression, and prejudice" (1977, 11).

7. Four years later, in *Sipuel v. Oklahoma Board of Regents* (1948), the Court summarily affirmed its holding in *Gaines* by holding that a law school admissions policy denying admission to racialized persons violated the Equal Protection Clause where there was no other way in the state for the petitioner to obtain the legal education that her qualifications warranted.

8. See Tex.Const., Art. VII, §§ 7, 14; Tex.Rev.Civ.Stat. (Vernon, 1925), Arts. 2643b (Supp. 1949), 2719, 2900.

9. See, for example, Virginia's Racial Integrity Act of 1924.

10. Since this action took place in the District of Columbia rather than in a state, the claim was that respondents' due process rights had been violated under the Fifth Amendment rather than their rights to equal protection under the Fourteenth Amendment.

11. For example, as was discussed above, the justification offered by the Supreme Court for creating Separate But Equal Doctrine in 1896 and then perpetuating it for fifty-eight years was that separate railway train accommodations, or separate water fountains, or separate schools for racialized persons were perfectly equal to the accommodations for nonracialized persons; and that such separate accommodations were not racist in virtue of this "equality."

12. See, for example, *Sheet Metal Workers v. Equal Employment Opportunity Commission* (1986).

13. See, for example, *Memphis Firefighters v. Stotts* (1984).

14. See, for example, *Martin v. Wilkes* (1989).

THREE

The Concept of Race and Equal Protection Law

Over the course of the development of equal protection law, roughly from 1868 (the year the Fourteenth Amendment to the U.S. Constitution, which contains the Equal Protection Clause, was ratified) to the present day, as the U.S. Supreme Court's concept of race moves from being understood as a sociocultural/sociohistorical phenomenon to being understood as a purely biological phenomenon, there is a concomitant shift on the part of the Court from understanding racial discrimination as problematic because it reinforces the legacy and vestiges of American chattel slavery, to understanding racial discrimination as problematic per se (U.S. Const. Amend. XIV § 1).[1] The Supreme Court's adoption, over time, of a purely biological concept of race is a curious state of affairs, given that academic thinking on the topic of race has taken the opposite turn during the same time period. That is, concurrent with the change in the Supreme Court's concept of race from sociocultural/sociohistorical to purely biological, the academic concept of race moves from being understood as purely biological to sociocultural/sociohistorical. Over the same period of time, nonracialized persons began to become successful at using the Equal Protection Clause to protect *them* from "racial discrimination." One explanation for this curious state of affairs may be that the current utilization by nonracialized Americans of the Equal Protection Clause for protection against "racial discrimination" is among the most recent examples of the progressive divestiture of the rights of racialized persons for the benefit of nonracialized persons, over time, in the United States since the end of the civil rights movement.

THE SUPREME COURT'S SWITCH FROM SOCIOCULTURAL/ SOCIOHISTORICAL RACE TO BIOLOGICAL RACE

To say that, in the nineteenth century, the Supreme Court understood race primarily as a sociocultural/sociohistorical phenomenon is to use contemporary terminology to describe a way of thinking about race that views race as deeply ensconced and invested in the cultural identity, history, and even geography of a given era. That is, the significance of race (its telos, its Aristotelian "function") had more to do with considerations of social structure, social mores, in-group/out-group psychology and power dynamics, than with phenotype, physiognomy, or physical characteristics (Aristotle, *NE*, 1.7). To be a member of one race or another, was a story about cultural belonging, and about the customs and laws of the country, including citizenship laws, federal naturalization laws, and Supreme Court decisions in which race was a factor. The nineteenth-century case law reveals that, for the Court at the time, blackness or whiteness as such, or per se, in the "philosophical void," as it were, did not exist. Instead, the Supreme Court correlated blackness and whiteness with geographical origins, traditions, and cultural narratives—that is, for example, with the sense of being "a people" in the Du Boisian sense (Du Bois 1897/2001).

While it is true, however, that even in the nineteenth century, the Supreme Court, at times, associated human racial categories with, among other things, heritability or "ancestry," the case reports reveal that there was no sense on the part of the Supreme Court in the nineteenth century or even the early twentieth century that race was a purely biological phenomenon, or that race could be separated from culture, history, or geography, in the way that the Court talks about race today.

Over time, however, the Supreme Court's concept of race changes. What can be seen in the case reports of Supreme Court cases grappling with the concept of race from the mid-nineteenth century to the present, in direct opposition with the trajectory of academic thinking on the topic, is a switch from understanding race in a sociocultural/sociohistorical way, to understanding race in a purely biological way in the late twentieth and early twenty-first centuries. To develop an appreciation for how the Supreme Court came to adopt a purely biological concept of race, it is helpful to take a close look at the language the Court has used in pivotal cases over the years in which race was at issue.

Early Supreme Court cases correlated human racial blackness with slavery, not with biology. This is true of both cases decided before the enactment of the Fourteenth Amendment and cases decided just afterwards. In the landmark *Dred Scott v. Sandford*, decided in 1857, eight years before the Civil War broke out and eleven years before the enactment of the Fourteenth Amendment, the plaintiff, Dred Scott is described as "a free Negro of the African race" whose ancestors had been brought to the United States and sold as slaves (*Dred Scott,* 1857, 393). The pivotal question in the case was whether Scott could avail himself of the court system. The Supreme Court held that he could not avail himself of the court system in virtue of the fact that he was not a citizen of the United States within the meaning of the U.S. Constitution.

The Court delved into the text of the Constitution for references to support its position. There were only two clauses in the Constitution that referred to persons such as Scott, the Court said, and in neither case were such persons considered citizens. Not being a citizen, Scott could not avail himself of the "special rights and immunities" guaranteed to citizens by the Constitution, including availing oneself of the court system (ibid.). By persons such as Scott, the Court explained that Scott's ancestors had never been intended to be citizens but only as property to be bought and sold. The Court wrote, "The question is simply this: Can a negro, whose ancestors were imported into this country, and sold as slaves, become a member of the political community formed and brought into existence by the Constitution of the United States, and as such become entitled to all the rights, and privileges, and immunities, guaranteed by that instrument to the citizen?" (ibid., 403). The Supreme Court's answer was no. In other words, Dred Scott was prohibited from filing suit in federal court not because of his so-called biological race *per se,* but because according to the Constitution, his ancestors were not citizens, but slaves.

Just after the enactment of the Fourteenth Amendment, the Supreme Court's concept of race vis-à-vis former slaves was no different.

In *The Slaughterhouse Cases* (1873), the Court wrote that since the Thirteenth Amendment was insufficient to protect "the colored race" from certain laws enacted in the southern states that imposed upon them "onerous disabilities and burdens and curtailing their rights in the pursuit of life, liberty, and property to such an extent that their freedom was of little value" (*The Slaughterhouse Cases,* 1873, 70), the Fourteenth Amendment was passed through Congress to provide additional protection for "the unfortunate race" who had "suffered so much" (ibid.). In *Slaughterhouse,* the facts of the case were that the Court denied nonracialized butchers the right to invoke the Equal Protection Clause of the Fourteenth Amendment to protect their interests.

The Court's rationale was that whatever were the nonracialized butchers' complaints, they had not experienced the denial of their rights in the same way that "the colored race" had as a result of the Jim Crow laws enacted after the end of slavery. To be "colored," in other words, meant that one was a member of a group with a pressing need to be protected by federal law from the infringement of one's rights by state laws designed to reinforce the badges of slavery. In a series of cases decided just after *The Slaughterhouse Cases,* the Court repeatedly associated being "colored" with having one's rights trampled on by invidious state laws in the aftermath of slavery. For example, in *Strauder v. West Virginia* (1880), the Court referred to racialized people as "a race recently emancipated" (*Strauder* 1880, 306); and in *The Civil Rights Cases* (1883), state laws were struck down that discriminated on the basis of any "previous condition of servitude" (*The Civil Rights Cases* 1883, 4).

The case of *Plessy v. Ferguson* (1896) brings into full focus the Court's understanding of race at the end of the nineteenth century. In that case, Homer Plessy was a person of "mixed descent" ("seven-eighths Caucasian and one eighth African blood" (*Plessy* 1896, 537) who possessed no obvious physical trait identified with racialized persons, i.e., "the mixture of colored blood was not discernible in him" (*Plessy* 1896, 537). Plessy had boarded a Louisiana train on the afternoon of June 7, 1892, for the purpose of taking a public stand against a Louisiana law mandating "equal but separate accommodations" for persons of "the white and colored races" on public conveyances. Upon boarding the train, no one stopped Plessy as he took his seat in first class, a section reserved exclusively for nonracialized persons. It was only after Plessy voluntarily and openly declared that under Louisiana law he was a "colored" man, that the conductor directed him to the colored car (Fireside 2004, 1). Plessy was charged with, and soon convicted of, breaking the Louisiana law.

Plessy appealed his conviction up through the Supreme Court of Louisiana, who held (as had all of the lower courts) that the Louisiana law was constitutional. In his appeal, Plessy challenged the constitutionality of the law to the Supreme Court. Reportedly, Plessy argued that owing to being seven-eighths Caucasian, he was "entitled to every right, privilege and immunity secured to citizens of the United States of the white race" (*Plessy* 1896, 541). The Court did not address Plessy's claims of being biologically "white" for all intents and purposes, but instead proceeded as if it were obvious that he was "black," and therefore in clear violation of the law. This could be attributable to the so-called "one drop rule," prevalent in Jim Crow laws of the time, but it is more likely attributable to the fact that the Court understood race as a sociocultural/sociohistorical phenomenon rather than a biological phenomenon. Plessy was "black" because that is the way he was understood by society, regardless of any talk of "blood."

Arguably, the most convincing proof that the *Plessy* Court was operating with a sociocultural/sociohistorical conception of race, however, is the fact that the Court is trying to uphold *social* distinctions and *social* segregation through its decision to uphold the Louisiana law. To reinforce this point, and referring to the power of the train conductor, the Court writes, "The power to assign to a particular coach obviously implies the power to determine to which race the passenger belongs, as well as the power to determine who, under the laws of the particular State, is to be deemed a white and who a colored person" (*Plessy* 1896, 549). In other words, the determination of "to which race the passenger belongs" is linked, in the Court's mind, to the discretion of the conductor and the power of the State, not to anything more theoretically "objective" like biology.

In the early twentieth century, various nonwhite persons other than "blacks" began to bring cases before the Supreme Court claiming that they were "white" and were therefore entitled to certain rights. The outcomes of these cases turned on the ethnoracial status of the persons bringing the cases before the Court, rather than on any biological test. An examination of the Supreme Court's reasoning process in these cases helps us get a clearer picture of how the Supreme Court thought about race at that time. In the following cases, which are typical of the time, the Court explicitly grapples with whether race should be understood to be biological or sociocultural/sociohistorical.

The first of the cases is *Ozawa v. United States* (1922). In *Ozawa,* a Japanese person wished to become a naturalized citizen. The Supreme Court held that Mr. Ozawa, having been born in Japan, did not qualify as a "free white person" under the federal naturalization laws, and therefore could not become a citizen of the United States (*Ozawa,* 1922, 194–99). Having been born in Japan meant that Mr. Ozawa was problematically not "Caucasian," the Court explained, and therefore not "white." Attempting to explain its reasoning process, the Court wrote, "[t]he intention [of the naturalization law] was to confer the privilege of citizenship upon that class of persons whom the [founding] fathers knew as white, and to deny it to those who could not be so classified" (*Ozawa,* 1922, 195). In other words, Mr. Ozawa was not "white" because he was not Caucasian, and he was not Caucasian because the founding fathers would not have wanted people like to Mr. Ozawa to be citizens. There is no mention, on the part of the Court, of Mr. Ozawa's "biology," phenotype, or physical features.

One year later, however, the Court decided that being "white" no longer turned on being Caucasian. In *U.S. v. Bhagat Sing Thind* (1923), when denying the status of "free white person" (for purposes of the same federal naturalization law) to a gentleman who had been born in India, the Court indicated that whether Mr. Thind was "Caucasian" or not was irrelevant. Explaining why qualifying as Caucasian was not sufficient for qualifying as "white" in this particular case, the Court wrote,

> [The word "Caucasian"] is at best a conventional term, with an altogether fortuitous origin, which under scientific manipulation, has come to include far more than the unscientific mind suspects. According to Keane, for example . . . it includes not only the Hindu, but some of the Polynesians . . . , the Hamites of Africa, upon the ground of the Caucasic cast of their features, though in color they range from brown to black. We venture to think that the average well-informed white American would learn with some degree of astonishment that the race to which he belongs is made up of such heterogeneous elements. . . . The various

authorities are in irreconcilable disagreement as to what constitutes a proper racial division. (211)

Having established that race was not susceptible to conclusive scientific analysis, and that the "average white American" was really the best judge of who was "white," the Court turns to the intent of the framers of the naturalization law, and to "words of familiar speech" to support its understanding of who qualifies as "white." The Court writes, "The words of familiar speech, which were used by the original framers of the law, were intended to include only the type of man whom they knew as white" (ibid., 213). The "white" group clearly includes, according to the Court, those "from the British Isles and Northwestern Europe" and those from Eastern, Southern, and Middle Europe and their descendants since these were the immigrants who "constituted the white population of the country" when the naturalization law was adopted (ibid., 214). The test for whiteness, according to the Court, was whether the nonracialized persons who drafted the naturalization laws would consider a given person "white" or not. The test for whiteness, as was the case in *Ozawa,* was the discretion of nonracialized persons, not biology.

Together, *Ozawa* and *Thind* seem to indicate that in 1923, to be "white" (at least for naturalization purposes) according to the Supreme Court, meant to be Caucasian when the person wishing to be considered "white" was Japanese, but meant the ordinary understanding of the term "white," when the person wishing to be considered "white" was Indian.

The third case, *Korematsu v. United States* (1944), was different in two important respects from *Ozawa* and *Thind*. Firstly, Korematsu was an American citizen of Japanese descent, instead of an immigrant, and second, rather than claiming that he should be considered "white" and therefore able to escape certain negative consequences for those deemed legally "nonwhite," claimed his right to equal protection had been denied by a federal evacuation order because of his race. Korematsu had been convicted in a federal court of remaining in San Leandro, California, contrary to an executive order directing that all persons of Japanese ancestry should be excluded from that area, and moved into internment camps after May 9, 1942. He appealed the conviction all the way to the Supreme Court. The Supreme Court concluded that the executive evacuation order did not violate Korematsu's right to equal protection, because the country's right to protect itself in time of war was more important than protecting Japanese Americans from racial discrimination.

On the topic of race, the *Korematsu* case was focused on persons of Japanese ancestry. In upholding the executive order, the Court stated that it was impossible to segregate loyal from disloyal Japanese Americans and cited information coming in from investigations that approximately five thousand American citizens of Japanese ancestry had refused to swear unqualified allegiance to the United States and to renounce allegiance to the Japanese emperor. On the topic of race, the Court repeatedly refers to "ancestry" and repeatedly states that the case is not about "racial prejudice" but about "military dangers": "Korematsu was not excluded from the Military Area because of hostility to him or his race. He was excluded because we are at war with the Japanese Empire . . . [among other non-race-related reasons]." Justice Roberts' dissenting opinion in this case would have found an equal protection violation, pointing out that Korematsu was forbidden in the relevant area "solely because of his ancestry" (*Korematsu* 1944, 226).

The relevant issues in *Korematsu* for answering the question of what the Supreme Court's concept of race was in the first part of the twentieth century are: (1) How, if at all, is the concept of race at work in *Korematsu* the same or different from the concept of race at work in *Ozawa* and *Thind*? (2) Is this concept more sociocultural/sociohistorical or biological? In all three cases, the relevant issue seems to be ancestry, that is, geographic origin. Moreover, the relevant test for who counts as what race seems to be the discretion of those either creating or implementing the laws, which is a subjective or social judgment rather than an objective biological determination. As the twentieth century wore on, and into the twenty-first century, the Court began to think about race in more biological terms, and eventually in biological terms divorced from considerations of history or social context.

In 1954, the Court decided two cases in which the concept of race was at issue, and in both cases took a kind of hybrid position on just exactly what race is. In the famous *Brown v. Board of Education*, discussed earlier, the Court is presented with the question of whether schools segregated along racial lines violate the Equal Protection Clause. Throughout its decision, the Court uses the terms "Negro" and "white" as if it is obvious to whom the Court is referring by these descriptive terms. However, in the course of the case, the Court holds that schools for "Negroes" causes "Negro"/"colored" children to develop a sense of inferiority, and that this is a deterrent to their ability to learn: "Whatever may have been the extent of psychological knowledge at the time of *Plessy v. Ferguson*, this finding is amply supported by modern authority. Any language in *Plessy v. Ferguson* contrary to this finding is rejected," the Court wrote (*Brown* 494/692). For this reason, the Court states, segregated schools violate "equal protection of the laws." If we unpack this language, as I suggested in the Introduction, the Court is saying that segregated schools *perpetuate the badges of slavery*. It was arguably obvious to everyone involved at the time, including the members of the Court, the attorneys, the litigants, and the general public, that (1) the schools racialized children were forced to attend were inferior, (2) one of the primary reasons the schools were inferior were that they were created to stigmatize and humiliate racialized children. *The fact of being separated off from other children, in other words, outside of the context of the history of chattel slavery and Jim Crow, would not, in and of itself, stigmatize.* It is safe to say, then, that the concept of race with which the Court is working here is unclear. On the one hand, the Court refers to "Negroes" and "white" children as if the difference between them is clear and obvious, usually indicating a "categorical" concept of race, which usually means biologically based (see, e.g., [Botts] Fernandes 2013; Leong 2010); but on the other hand the Court implicitly recognizes the sociocultural/sociohistorical concept of race in its rationale for *why* racially segregated schools violate equal protection of the laws *for racialized children* in 1954 in the United States, i.e., because being a racialized person in the United States in 1954 meant that when one is separated off from the general population on racial grounds, the reason for the separation is almost certainly to stigmatize and humiliate.

The lesser known, but equally interesting, 1954 case of *Hernandez v. Texas* is similarly ambiguous on the concept of race. In *Hernandez,* the petitioner, Pete Hernandez was indicted for murder in Jackson County, Texas. He was convicted and sentenced to life imprisonment. The Texas Court of Criminal Appeals affirmed the judgment of the trial court. But, prior to the trial, Hernandez, through counsel, claimed that persons of Mexican descent were systematically excluded from service as jurors, although there were many such persons who were qualified to be jurors in the relevant community. Mr. Hernandez claimed that the exclusion of such persons from jury membership deprived him of equal protection of the laws. The Supreme Court agreed.

> In numerous decisions, this Court has held that it is a denial of the equal protection of the laws to try a defendant of a particular race or color under an indictment issued by a grand jury . . . from which all persons of his race or color have, solely because of that race or color, been excluded by the State. (*Hernandez* 477/670)

In *Hernandez,* although the Court seems to be equating race with "color," implicating the utilization of a biological (or at least phenotypical) concept of race, at the same time the Court implicitly articulates the utilization of a sociocultural/sociohistorical concept of race through stating that it is an equal protection violation of the rights of a criminal defendant to have jurors of his (or her) own "race or color" systematically excluded from the jury. In other words, through that decision, the Court arguably invokes the sociohistorical context in which juries that exclude jurors of one's own race are usually biased against the defendant (within a racialized society with a history of racialized hierarchy). The fact that the Court rejected the State's claim that it had not discriminated against persons of Mexican descent in jury selection, but had only selected "those whom they thought were best qualified" (despite conclusive evidence submitted that in the previous twenty-five years there was no record of any person with a Mexican or Latin American name having served on a jury), substantiates the sociocultural reading: "[I]t taxes our credulity to say that mere chance resulted in there being no members of this class [persons of Mexican decent] among the over six thousand jurors called in the past 25 years," the Court wrote (*Hernandez* 482/672).

More evidence of the sociocultural/sociohistorical reading is arguably to be found in the manner in which the identity of being a person of Mexican descent was handled by the Court in *Hernandez*. The Court stated that in order to reach its finding that Mr. Hernandez's equal protection rights had been violated by the jury selection, Mr. Hernandez first had to prove that "persons of Mexican descent [constituted] a separate class in Jackson County (Texas), *distinct from 'whites'*" (*Hernandez* 479/671). "One method by which this may be demonstrated is by showing the attitude of the community," the Court continued (ibid.). The testimony of "responsible officials and citizens" was consulted to address this issue, who confirmed that "[t]he participation of persons of Mexican descent in business and community groups was shown to be slight" (ibid.). Moreover, "until very recent times" (in the case), children "of Mexican descent" were required to attend segregated schools for the first four grades. Additionally, at least one restaurant in town "prominently" displayed a sign stating, "No Mexicans served." Finally, there were two men's toilets on the courthouse grounds, one unmarked and one marked "Colored Men" and "Hombres Aqui" ("Men Here") (ibid.). All of this would seem to indicate that the Court is utilizing a sociocultural/sociohistorical concept of race in its decision, despite its utilization of "race" and "color" interchangeably in the case.

Substantially contributing to the trend of the Supreme Court's beginning to think about race in biological rather than sociocultural/sociohistorical terms, however, was a line of reasoning regarding the concept of *immutability* that entered into the equal protection discussion through cases of discrimination against women. In *Frontiero v. Richardson* (1973), the Supreme Court concluded, in a plurality decision, that discrimination on the basis of sex (what we now call gender) was unconstitutional for the reason that "sex, like race and national origin [was] an 'immutable characteristic'" (*Frontiero* 1973, 686) such that discrimination on the basis of sex (what we now call gender) "would seem to violate the basic concept of our system that legal burdens should bear some relationship to individual responsibility" (ibid.).

This "immutable characteristic" language (which implicated that race was based in biology and this was the reason that racial discrimination was problematic), then moved from a case addressing discrimination against women (i.e., *Frontiero*) to cases addressing racial discrimination. It is important that at no point prior to *Frontiero* had the Court stated that the "immutable characteristic" of blackness (and certainly not the "immutable characteristic" of race) was a constitutionally impermissible basis upon which to legally discriminate against persons. However, beginning with *Regents of the University of California v. Bakke* (1978), the Court began to reason in these terms, that is, it began to use the concept of the immutability of race in its reasoning process. In subsequent cases, the Court continues to speak of race as if it were "immutable," see, for example, *Fullilove v. Klutznick* (1980), and eventually speaks as if the immutability and purely biological nature of race are obvious and not in need of justification or explanation.

THE ACADEMIC SWITCH FROM BIOLOGICAL RACE TO SOCIOCULTURAL/SOCIOHISTORICAL RACE

In direct contrast to the trajectory of Supreme Court thinking on the concept of race, the academic concept of race started out in the nineteenth century—at least in European thought—as an understanding of race as a biological phenomenon and then moved, particularly in the past seventy-five years or so, into an understanding of race as a purely sociocultural/sociohistorical phenomenon. It is widely accepted that leading theorists of race in the late eighteenth century, such as Immanuel Kant and Johann Friedrich Blumenbach, generated the concept of biologically based human races, relying on travelogues provided by travelers involved in missionary work, colonization, and the slave trade for their information (Bernasconi & Lott, 2000). Based on these travelogues, Kant's "Of the Different Human Races," for example, is commonly understood as the first attempt to provide a "scientific" definition of race, according to which there were four biologically based human races: "white," "Negro," "Hun," and "Hindu" (Kant, 2000, 11). Interestingly, under the Kantian schema, the distinction between "Negroes and whites" was "self-evident" (Kant, 2000, 12). The 1781 version of Blumenbach's "On the Natural Variety of Mankind" added a fifth biological race (although the term he used was not "race" but "variety"), so the list of races became: "Causasian," "Ethiopian," "Mongolian," "Malay," and "American," each with an associated "colour" (Blumenbach, 2000, 27).

Based on this eighteenth-century, academic concept of race as biologically based, as time went on, what I will call the traditional folk concept of race developed, according to which race was also biological. This conception of race is very popular even today in the United States, according to which human racial categories are real, biologically based, pure, and exist in a hierarchy, with nonracialized persons at the top of the hierarchy and racialized persons at the bottom. A key feature of the traditional folk concept of race is that there are, at bottom, only two races: "white" and "black." This unique feature of American racial consciousness is sometimes referred to as the "black-white binary" (Sundstrom 2008). The traditional folk concept of race, however, fell out of favor in the academic community starting in the mid-twentieth century, and is still out of favor in academia today (see Montagu 1942; UNESCO 1951; Livingstone, 1962; Lewontin 1972; Hubbard and Wald 1999; Graves 2001).

Within the discipline of philosophy, and over the past thirty-five years or so (particularly within the critical philosophy of race), in the aftermath of the general consensus in the scientific community since roughly the 1950s that biological race does not refer to anything in the world, several more viable concepts of race have developed. These are that (1) race is not real and there is no such thing as race; (2) race is real and is based in biology, but does not carry with it the concepts of racial purity or a hierarchy of the races; (3) race is real, but is a social kind rather than a biological kind, that is, race is socially constructed. Charles Mills calls these three philosophically viable concepts of race (1) eliminativism/error theory, (2) racial biologism, and (3) anti-eliminativist constructionism, respectively (Mills 2014, 89).

A bit of additional detail on these three metaphysical positions on the concept of race adds insight. Eliminativism is the view, generally, that since the word "race" has no referent, we should stop using it. Kwame Anthony Appiah and Naomi Zack were the early proponents of this view (Appiah 1992, Zack 1994). "Racial biologism," as Mills defines it, is the view that a biological concept of race can (and by implication, should) be retained that does not carry with it some of the less palatable aspects of traditional, biological race such as a hierarchy among the races (see, e.g., Spencer 2012); and "anti-eliminativist constructionism" is the view, generally, that race is a social kind rather than a natural kind (Mills 2014, 89). Further distinctions are sometimes made between strong and weak constructionism. In broad strokes, "strong" constructionism entails the belief that race has a metaphysical referent in the world (or multiple metaphysical referents), whereas "weak" constructionism does not entail this claim (see Atkin 2012, 57–71). In both cases, however, biologically based ontology is dropped. While there is controversy within the discipline of philosophy over which of these three metaphysical positions is the most convincing, outside of philosophy almost all academic disciplines accept the weak social constructionist account of race, according to which race is a purely sociocultural/sociohistorical (contingent, context-dependent) phenomenon.

A CHANGE IN UNDERSTANDING OF THE PROBLEM OF RACIAL DISCRIMINATION

As the change in the Court's thinking about race takes place from sociocultural/sociohistorical to biological, the Equal Protection Clause moves, vis-à-vis racial discrimination, from being understood as a remedial measure to curb the vestiges of chattel slavery, to a device for protecting everyone, regardless of racial identification, from "racial discrimination."

Thus, while the early Supreme Court cases interpreting the Fourteenth Amendment stressed the remedial purpose of the Equal Protection Clause in light of the problem of the continued subordination of racialized persons after the Civil War, as time went on, the cases began to back away from this remedial purpose of the Clause, and simultaneously began to equate racial discrimination with differentiating on the basis of race at large. This can be understood as a kind of whitewashing of the Equal Protection Clause, in the sense that the historical purpose of the Clause as a remedy available to descendants of slavery for very specific reasons was no longer discussed.

The Equal Protection Clause of the Fourteenth Amendment to the United States Constitution was placed into the Amendment as a remedial measure for the purpose of providing a means for racialized persons to challenge state-enacted laws that either reinforced or perpetuated what the Supreme Court called the "badges of slavery" after the end of the Civil War. The Congressional debates that took place in 1866 during the 39th Congress bear this fact out. When Congressman Stevens introduced the Amendment in the House, he characterized its purpose as "the amelioration of the condition of the freedmen" (Cong. Globe, 39th Cong., 1st Sess. 2459, 1866). Additionally, proponents of the Fourteenth Amendment repeatedly emphasized that one of the Amendment's primary purposes was to place in the Constitution itself, the principles of Section 1 of the Civil Rights Act of 1866. The purpose of this Act was to give citizens "without regard to race and color, without regard to any previous condition of slavery or involuntary servitude . . . full and equal benefit of all laws and proceedings for the security of person and property, as is enjoyed by white citizens" (Civil Rights Act of 1866). Proponents of the Fourteenth Amendment in the early Congressional debates repeatedly stated that the Fourteenth Amendment's primary purpose was to address the manifest unequal status of racialized persons as a group. Therefore, the historical evidence shows that rather than being designed to address racial discrimination as such, "the [Congressional] debates reveal overriding concern with the status of one racial group [i.e., racialized persons]" (Baer 1983, 138).

The enactment of the Thirteenth, Fourteenth, and Fifteenth Amendments to the U.S. Constitution, known collectively as the Civil War Amendments, mirrored the purpose of the Civil Rights Act of 1866. In December of 1865, the Thirteenth Amendment, which banned slavery everywhere in the United States, was ratified (Rawley 1989). Two and a half years later, in July 1868, the Fourteenth Amendment (containing the Equal Protection Clause) was ratified, and then about two years after that, in March of 1870, the Fifteenth Amendment, prohibiting discrimination in voting "on account of race, color, or previous condition of servitude," was ratified. Taken together, these Civil War Amendments suggest that the Equal Protection Clause was included in the Fourteenth

Amendment to make clear that equal protection under the law for racialized Americans could and would be federally enforced. Accordingly, Justice Miller stated in the 1873 *Slaughterhouse Cases* that the Fourteenth Amendment had "one pervading purpose," which was "the protection of the newly made freeman and citizen from the oppressions of those who had formerly exercised unlimited dominion over him" (*Slaughterhouse,* 1873, 71).

The *Korematsu* case represents a turning point. In addition to identifying Japanese Americans as a "racial group," the *Korematsu* case also held that all legal restrictions which curtail the civil rights of a "single racial group" were immediately suspect and should be subjected to "the most rigid scrutiny" (*Korematsu,* 1944, 216). In other words, the *Korematsu* Court suggested that the Equal Protection Clause should be understood or interpreted to provide special protection for a "racial group" (whatever that concept might entail) when a given law negatively impacted the rights of that group qua group. With this case, the Court began to find legalized racial discrimination problematic in itself, rather than problematic when directed toward a specific "racial" group, specifically the descendants of slaves.

In the late twentieth century, the concept of immutability entered into the Supreme Court's understanding of the concept of race, and began to affect how the Court understood racial discrimination. That is, the Court began to use the supposed immutability of race to support its position that all racial classifications were invidious, even those that disadvantaged nonracialized persons, and all racial classifications were therefore in violation of the Equal Protection Clause. The Court's reasoning in *Regents of the University of Californa v. Bakke* (1978) is typical. Whiteness is just as immutable as blackness, the Court reasoned, such that a classification that disadvantages nonracialized persons is no more constitutional than a classification which disadvantages racialized persons. Justice Rehnquist's dissent in *United Steelworkers v. Weber* (1979) is also typical of the time period: "The evil inherent in discrimination against Negroes is that it is based on an immutable characteristic. . . . The characteristic becomes no less immutable and irrelevant, *and discrimination based thereon becomes no less evil,* simply because the person excluded is a member of one race rather than another," he wrote (*United Steelworkers,* 1979, 255; emphasis added).

The recent cases of *Gratz v. Bollinger*, 539 U.S. 244 (2003) and *Grutter v. Bollinger*, 539 U.S. 306 (2003), collectively known as "the Michigan cases" solidified the Court's transition to understanding racial discrimination as problematic per se. The result is that equal protection law currently protects nonracialized Americans more often than racialized Americans from "racial discrimination," and leaves racialized Americans largely unprotected by the Equal Protection Clause.

CONCLUDING REFLECTIONS

The Supreme Court's contemporary understanding of the concept of race as a purely biological phenomenon is in direct contrast to contemporary academic thinking on the topic of race, which understands race as a sociocultural/sociohistorical phenomenon. Moreover, the Court's switch from a sociocultural/sociohistorical (or, in philosophical terms, a social constructionist) concept of race to a purely biological concept of race during the same period of time that the academic concept of race reverses itself in the opposite direction is a curious state of affairs, given that the result is that the Equal Protection Clause, vis-à-vis racial discrimination, has moved from a device to protect racialized Americans to a device that protects primarily nonracialized Americans.

One explanation for this state of affairs is that the appropriation by nonracialized Americans of the usage of the Equal Protection Clause for protection against "racial discrimination" is part of the larger phenomenon of the divestiture of the rights of racialized persons for the benefits of nonracialized persons over time since the end of the civil rights movement. Arguably, were the Court to follow academic wisdom and utilize a sociocultural/sociohistorical concept of race rather than a biological one, it would then have to confront that racial discrimination is not something that happens in a vacuum. It would have to confront that racial discrimination does not mean, as some scholars contend, behaving as if race were important when it isn't. Instead, racial discrimination is something that occurs in a context in which the vestiges or "badges" of slavery are not a thing of the past, but are perpetuated through policies and laws that treat racialized persons as less "equal" than nonracialized persons. The Supreme Court's present reliance on a purely biological concept of race at virtually the same point in time as the biological concept of race is dropped from academic legitimacy is therefore both anomalous and disturbing.

NOTE

1. This chapter consists of extracts from pp. 526–36, Ch. 44, "The Concept of Race and Equal Protection Law," by Tina Botts from "Oxford Handbook of Philosophy and Race," edited by Naomi Zack, 2017, reprinted here by permission of Oxford University Press.

FOUR

The Concept of Equality and Equal Protection Law

In chapter 3, I explained how the Supreme Court's switch from interpreting the Equal Protection Clause as designed to protect racialized persons to interpreting the Clause as designed to eliminate racial discrimination per se was accompanied by a concomitant shift in the Supreme Court's concept of race (i.e., from sociocultural to biological). In chapter 4, I will show that, over the same time period, there was also a shift in the Court's concept of equality (i.e., from social equality to legal equality). To help provide structure to the chapter—that is, to provide a framework of meaning within which to conduct the investigation—I will work with four main concepts of equality, as developed by David Johnston.[1] For Johnston, the four main concepts of equality in Western juridicopolitical thought are: moral equality, legal equality, political equality, and social equality (see Johnston 2000, vii).[2] For Johnston, *moral equality* is the idea that people are of equal value or worth, or that they should be regarded as being of equal value or worth; *legal equality* is the idea that the law should be applied impartially to all people; *political equality* is the idea that all members of a political community should have an equal say in things; and *social equality* is the idea that all people should enjoy equal access to basic social goods such as flourishing lives, income, wealth, health care, education, and jobs.

More specifically, what I will show in chapter 4 is that while *social* equality was the form of equality motivating the push to include the Equal Protection Clause in the Fourteenth Amendment, and while early Supreme Court decisions interpreting the Clause were mindful of the goal of social equality, by the time we reach the late twentieth century, the Court interprets the Clause as if it operates in the service of *legal* equality.[3] At the same time, I will also make the case that there are (at least) two problems with using legal equality (rather than social equality) to guide equal protection law. First, using legal equality to guide equal protection law is out of step with both the purpose of the Clause and the demands of the contemporary context, and second, using legal equality to guide equal protection law actually facilitates and perpetuates, rather than alleviates, the problem of inequality based on race in the United States.

EARLY EQUAL PROTECTION LAW: SOCIAL EQUALITY

Social equality was the form of equality guiding early equal protection law. Recall that for David Johnston *social equality* is the idea that all people should enjoy equal access to basic social goods such as flourishing lives, income, wealth, health care, education, and jobs. Carina Fourie embellishes on this definition, taking it a bit deeper, arguing that social equality is a significant and distinct, yet neglected (in philosophical scholarship) component of what it means to be equals (Fourie 2011). For Fourie, while discussions of equality in contemporary philosophy focus primarily on the role of equality in distributive justice, or what can be termed "distributive equality," distinctively *social* equality has more to do with equality per se. Citing David Miller, Fourie writes that a society marked by social equality would be one that is not marked by status divisions such that one can place different people in hierarchically ranked categories or different classes (Miller 1998; Fourie 2011, 110). An opposition to ranking people according to hierarchies of social status "appears to be *the* central tenet of social equality," writes Fourie (111), such that an absence of status hierarchies would mark a socially equal society. A status hierarchy, Fourie explains, occurs when a social practice or policy expresses an unequal relationship between persons, or between groups of people, of inferiors and superiors.

To help us picture what status hierarchy (and hence, social inequality) looks like, Fourie provides us with the example of how racialized persons in the United States were at one time expected to step off the pavement to get out of the way of approaching nonracialized persons. Another example of status/social inequality, according to Fourie, is the fact that in apartheid South Africa, racialized persons were expected to call nonracialized males "Baas" (meaning "Boss") and nonracialized females "Madam," while at the same time nonracialized persons would often refer to adult racialized persons as "boy" or "girl." Social equality, then, for Fourie, expresses the opposite of such situations, articulating "an ideal where people stand in equal relation to each other rather than being treated better or worse, inferior or superior" (Fourie 2011, 112). Fourie elaborates by observing that the point of identifying social equality (as distinct from inequalities of income distribution, power or political participation, for example) is to stress that there is an equality violation in—to use our example—having to get out of someone else's way merely because one belongs to one group and they to another "*even if there are no other violations of justice associated with this inequality*" (emphasis added) (Fourie 2011, 108). Fourie stresses that her status inequality (as a form of social inequality) is usually accompanied by other forms of (social) inequality like inequality of resources, welfare, and capabilities, but she suggests that *at the bottom of all of these forms* is the kind of inequality that amounts to inequality per se, or status inequality.[4]

Importantly, for Fourie, it is possible for social inequality (defined as inequality of status or "status inequality" or "status hierarchy") to be built into the formal legal and political framework of a society. She cites the caste system in India; the system of racial classification in apartheid South Africa; and the hierarchy of slaves, metics (resident aliens), and citizens in Ancient Greece as examples. Social inequality thus defined need not be legally coded and coercively enforced, however. It is often simply a part of the social structure of a given society. Moreover, according to Fourie, since theories of distributive justice emphasize the justice of institutions, they are often silent about the informal social inequalities of civil life. For this reason, it may be that distributive justice neglects what is likely a significant element of a society of equals, and that is an egalitarian *ethos*.

An examination of the harmful consequences of status inequality, according to Fourie, reinforces the wisdom of incorporating status equality into an egalitarian ethos. Within a system teeming with status inequality, the harms to those deemed inferior by status hierarchy are arguably obvious. The harms to those deemed superior may not be as obvious, but are nevertheless intuitively likely. These include, according to Fourie (who draws upon interdisciplinary research): (1) impaired moral capacity, resulting in a lack of empathy and inhumanity, (2) cognitive distortion, "leading to self-deception, as it may be necessary to develop a false notion of reality and a distorted conception of self and others in order to maintain belief in the 'justice' of the social system . . . in the face of the humiliation and degradation of others" (Fourie 2011, 120), (3) emotional costs such as heightened stress, anxiety, and aggression. Indeed, along certain dimensions of well-being, those with higher status equality may be as bad off as those with the lower within a system of status inequality. For example, Fourie asks us to consider what Martha Nussbaum refers to as "affiliation," defined as "being able to live with and towards others, to recognize and show concern for other human beings, to engage in various forms of social interaction, to be able to imagine the situation of another and to have compassion for that situation; to have the capability for both justice and friendship" (Nussbaum 2000, 79; Fourier 2011, 212). For Fourie, in a society lacking in status equality, those deemed superior will have a difficult time with affiliation, and lead lives of significantly diminished well-being as a result.

Charles Mills is arguably speaking of a form of social/status equality when he argues that what he calls "racial equality" is undertheorized in the discipline of philosophy (Mills 2015). The way Mills sees it, given the centrality of race and racial inequality to modernity, "racial equality as an achieved reality would have far reaching implications that would dramatically reshape the world" (43). To help us understand why racial equality is undertheorized philosophically but central to an understanding of modernity, Mills first reframes the issue of racial equality in such a way as to address the misleading way race and racism are framed in mainstream social justice theory, particularly Rawlsianism. First, Mills makes clear that he is an "anti-eliminativist constructionist" about race. To him, that means that although he understands races as socially constructed, he nonetheless accepts them as real, and specifically as brought into existence through discriminatory sociopolitical processes.[5] Next, Mills explains that he accepts a "doxastic" analysis of racism, according to which racism is best seen as a matter of beliefs, with these beliefs being, at a minimum that (1) the human race is divided into discrete races, (2) some races are superior to others, and (3) this superiority is based on distinctive traits and tendencies of the superior and inferior races (46). Finally, Mills tells us that racism is sociostructural, by which he means that race is deeply imbedded in the social and institutional structures of Western democracies (like the United States). Moreover, "the reality of systemic racial inequality," for Mills, "overturns Rawls's seemingly innocuous—but actually deeply theoretically loaded and misleading—assumption of a polity constructed by political equals undifferentiated by race" (50).

Explaining more fully what he means by social equality along racial lines or "racial equality," Mills proposes four senses of the concept: (1) racial equality as ontological, (2) racial equality as capability, (3) racial equality as norm of treatment, and (4) racial equality as social goal. Regarding ontological, racial equality, Mills has this to say: "If modernity is supposed to eliminate the hierarchies of the pre-modern Western world, the reality is that it only does so (to the extent that it does) for white males" (Mills 2015, 50). "[F]or hundreds of years," Mills writes, "and arguably even now to a certain extent, people of color were not seen by whites as full persons" (51). Regarding the first sense of racial equality, i.e., racial equality as ontological, Mills says that some people within liberalism are more ontologically equal than others (i.e., nonracialized persons over racialized persons). Regarding the second sense of racial equality, i.e., racial equality as capability, Mills defines racial equality as capability as having to do with the claim that although racial *potentials* are equal, *achieved* potentials vary because of "cultural" traits. If the long-standing gap between average nonracialized and racialized IQ test scores is explained not by cultural bias in the tests or inferior educational resources for racialized persons, or huge wealth differentials between racialized and nonracialized households, but by "cultural" differences, then the differences are differences in capabilities, such that the gap between innate and achieved potential as a goal is outside the scope of appropriate state remediation.[6] Regarding racial equality as norm of treatment, Mills states that this form of racial equality is effectively the same thing as color-blindness. Although since the advent of color-blindness "[c]rucial racial indicators are not only *not improving* but in some cases getting worse," this is not interpreted as ongoing racial injustice perpetrated by the nonracialized but to "ongoing . . . fecklessness" on the part of the racialized. Finally, regarding racial equality as social equality, Mills describes it as "usually measured by R1/R2 disproportionality in the relevant social statistics" where R1 and R2 represent two different races (impliedly racialized and nonracialized persons) (55).

It is this fourth sense of equality (what I am calling social equality) with which Mills is primarily concerned. Mills emphasizes that racial inequality as social inequality is largely untreated in philosophy, and ignored by social justice literature "across the liberal spectrum, from right wing market liberalism . . . to left-wing social democratic liberalism" (Mills 2015, 57–58). To change this state of affairs, Mills thinks we need to start from "the exit from ideal theory" (58) for the reason that ideal theory "has itself become a central obstacle to discussing and realizing racial justice" (59). For, "a racialized society is not slightly but *radically* different from [the ideal of a perfectly just society]," a society "conceived of . . . as a cooperative venture for mutual advantage" (59). Where reciprocity should be in a perfectly just society (of the Rawlsian variety), "a dominant system of racialized contempt" exists in its place, for Mills (ibid.).

I will say more about Mills's recommended "exit from ideal theory," as a solution to the problem of racial inequality, in chapter 6. What I want to stress here in chapter 4, on the concept of equality, is that the kind of equality that is necessary to undermine the current liberal/neoliberal system of "racialized contempt" (i.e., banal but ever-present and dangerous inequality along racial lines) is social equality, also known as equality of status, which means an absence of social hierarchy grounded in race.[7] Samuel Scheffler calls the kind of equality at issue "relational" equality (Scheffler 2015). "According to the . . . relational view [of equality]," Scheffler writes, "equality is an ideal governing certain kinds of interpersonal relationships" (21). Scheffler continues, "It plays a central role in political philosophy because justice requires the establishment of a society of equals, a society whose members relate to one another on a footing of equality" (ibid.). Moreover, and even more pointedly, "[T]he relational view is not a version of but is rather a genuine alternative to the distributive view" (ibid.). "In a relationship that is conducted on a footing of equality, each person accepts that the other person's equally important interests—understood broadly to include the person's needs, values, and preferences—should play an *equally significant role* in influencing decisions made within the context of the relationship. Moreover, each person has a normally effective disposition to *treat the other's interests accordingly*" (Scheffler 2015, 25, emphasis added).

Also theorizing racial inequality as a form of social inequality, Chris Lebron, in *The Color of Our Shame,* seeks a normative framework that justifies and motivates actions and dispositions that produce racially distinct outcomes. This framework Lebron calls the *problem of social value,* defined as "the fact that blacks do not occupy an equal place in the scheme of normative attention and concern upon which our society depends in the first place to justify the distribution of benefits and burdens, as well as to identify those who are deserving or appropriate recipients" (Lebron 2015, 46). The problem of social value, for Lebron, indicates that our social practices, "embedded as they are within a liberal democratic framework, are *outwardly* regulated by rules and principles meant to preempt categorical inequalities, but fail selectively—that is, in the face of race" (139).

In summary, then, and according to the theorists above, social equality is the idea that all people should enjoy equal access to basic social goods such as flourishing lives, income, wealth, health care, education, and jobs. Social equality is arguably distinct from distributive justice or distributive equality, however, in that it has more to do with a rejection of status hierarchy than with economic concerns or the (re)distribution of social goods. There is social inequality where there is hierarchy or inequality of status in society. Social inequality can be built into the formal legal and political framework (like in apartheid South Africa or the Jim Crow south in the United States), but it need not be. It is enough to make it disturbingly problematic that it exists in the social structure of a given society, in the relationships between persons. Social inequality is obviously harmful to members of lower status groups, but also harmful to members of higher status groups a well.[8] Social equality as between racial groups can be termed racial equality. Its opposite is racial inequality. Racial inequality (as social inequality) highlights some dents in the armor of liberal political theory. Specifically, to the extent that liberal political theory is ideal theory (understood as highly abstract and out of touch with the daily realities of lived experience), it is racist and generates social inequality. Social inequality along racial lines can also be thought of as the problem of social value, defined very simply as the fact that racialized persons not only *do not* occupy an equal place in the scheme of normative attention and concern, they are also not identified as deserving or appropriate recipients of society's benefits in the first place.

As mentioned at the top of this chapter, the early Supreme Court decisions interpreting the Equal Protection Clause understood social equality as the goal of the Clause. Recall from chapter 2 that in *The*

Slaughterhouse Cases (1873), decided eight years after the end of the Civil War and five years after the enactment of the Fourteenth Amendment, several nonracialized butchers were unable to obtain injunctions in state courts against enforcement of a state statute that gave to one of the slaughterhouses a monopoly for the city of New Orleans. The butchers claimed that the Louisiana law denied them equal protection of the laws. In its reasoning, the Court observed that the Fourteenth Amendment was intended to protect former slaves only. The Court in this case was arguably concerned to preserve the utilization of the Equal Protection Clause for the remediation of the wrong done to former slaves and their progeny, still suffering inequality after the end of slavery and the war. To utilize the Clause to protect nonracialized butchers as a class was not in line with that social goal.

Recall also that in *Strauder v. West Virginia* (1880), the Court stated that the Clause was designed to protect former slaves, and was there to protect racialized persons ("the colored race") from discrimination against them on the basis of their status as racialized persons. The Fourteenth Amendment, the Court stated in *Strauder,* was intended to secure to racialized persons all of the civil rights enjoyed by others, in addition to conferring a positive immunity or exemption for racialized persons from all discrimination which implied legal inferiority, which lessened the security of their rights, or which amounted to an attempt to reduce them to a condition of a subject race. The concern in each of these cases was rectification of the grave wrong done to racialized persons during the institution of chattel slavery, the continuing wrong being done to former slaves and their descendants by laws designed to perpetuate the severely low social status to which racialized persons were assigned as a result of slavery, and the desire to provide a remedy to racialized persons when states attempted to formalize or perpetuate the low social status of racialized persons by enacting laws to accomplish these purposes.

CONTEMPORARY EQUAL PROTECTION LAW: LEGAL EQUALITY

Legal equality, rather than social equality, is the form of equality guiding recent Supreme Court decisions. Often termed "formal equality," legal equality requires that the law should be applied to all people in an impartial way. However, the effect of utilizing legal equality to address the problems of an unequal world is the perpetuation of social inequality. To make this point, I will show that legal equality (1) can be traced back to Aristotle's proportional equality, according to which equality is available for "equals" only and not for "unequals," (2) develops and extends into Enlightenment political thought, particularly Social Contract Theory, (3) was never meant to operate to address problems like the problem of racial inequality, and (4) arguably cannot address the problem of racial inequality.

Legal equality has its origins in Aristotle's theory of justice. Justice, for Aristotle, describes conduct in agreement with the "law." In the *Nicomachean Ethics,* Aristotle states that justice is the greatest moral virtue, noting that justice is a sort of equality. Equality, Aristotle states, however, is available for equals but not for unequals. Aristotle explains that justice means treating like cases alike (Arist. *NE* V.3., 1131a10–b15, trans. Peters). In this way, for Aristotle, "that which is just is in some sort proportionate" (Arist. *NE* V.3, 8–9, trans. Peters). Aristotle continues, "That which is just, then, in this sense is that which is proportionate; but that which is unjust is that which is disproportionate" (Arist. *NE* V.3, 17–19, trans. Peters). In the *Politics,* Aristotle follows up on what justice is and its relationship to equality. Once again, Aristotle reminds us that we should treat like cases alike (Arist. *Pol.* III.9, 1280a8–15, trans. Irwin & Fine). He also tells us that the essence of justice is equality, though not for everyone, only for those who are equals. For Aristotle, equals should be treated equally and unequals unequally (Arist. *Pol.* III.9, 1280a11–15, trans. Irwin & Fine). In general, this language is interpreted as standing for the proposition that justice requires that *insofar as persons are the same in morally relevant respects,* they should be treated the same, and *insofar as they differ in those respects,* they should be treated differently (Feinberg 1980, Westen 1990, Raz 1986). I will refer to this conception of equality as Aristotle's "proportional equality."

Aristotle develops his proportional equality in conjunction with his complex and internally variable account of the ideal city-state or polis, which is, in turn, firmly rooted in his philosophy of nature (Taylor, 1995, 235). On the one hand, Aristotle says that the best city-state is one in which every citizen has the opportunity to achieve excellence of intellect and character; but, on the other hand, Aristotle specifies the development of intellect and character to require a lifestyle in which the necessities of life are provided by others. Those who provide the necessities of life are not included in Aristotle's vision of a kind of natural equality for all citizens, in other words, and neither is the development of intellect and character available to them.

Relatedly, there is much discussion in the *Politics* of the relationship of master and slave, which Aristotle regards as a natural relationship. Aristotle explains, "[A] slave, then, is a particular sort of animate tool" (Arist. *Pol.* I.4, 1253b32–33, trans. Irwin & Fine). For him, there are natural slaves, i.e., those who cannot survive without masters: "For someone is a natural slave if he is capable of belonging to another (that is why he belongs to another)" (Arist. *Pol.* I.5, 1254b22–23, Irwin & Fine). No equality is due to natural slaves, for they lack the ability to engage in practical reasoning and are inherently not self-possessed. Aristotle continues,

"[T]he slave not only is the slave of the master, but also belongs altogether to the master" (Arist. *Pol.* I.4, 1254a12–13, trans. Irwin & Fine). Describing those who are natural slaves, Aristotle writes,

> "[T]hose who are as different from normal human beings as body is from soul, or beast from human being—and this is the condition of those whose function and best product is the use of their body—these are natural slaves, and it is better for them . . . to be ruled by a master's rule" (Arist. *Pol.* I.5, 1254b17–21, trans. Irwin & Fine). "It is evident, then," Aristotle concludes, "that some are naturally free, others natural slaves; and for natural slaves slavery is both expedient and just." (Arist. *Pol.* I.5, 1255a40–41, trans. Irwin & Fine)

In summary, for Aristotle, then, in the *Nicomachean Ethics* and the *Politics,* justice (or legal equality) is a form of equality, according to which equality is available for equals but not for unequals. This is because justice is providing everyone with what they are due. "Natural" slaves are naturally unequal, owing to their inferior intellect and being primarily useful for manual labor ("the use of their body"), and are accordingly entitled to an unequal share of justice. Because Aristotle permits, or even requires, inequality if it reflects a difference in worth, some argue that Aristotle is a meritocrat (i.e., he assigns shares of equality based on merit). However, the extent to which proportional equality justifies inequality, for Aristotle, depends upon what Aristotle takes to be the grounds of worth (or merit). Based on his discussion of the relationship between master and slave (and, incidentally between husband and wife, males and females), Aristotle takes differences in worth (or merit) to be a function of nature.

Aristotle's proportional equality is central to his theory of justice, according to which inequality results when each does not get what is due. Legal equality (or justice) obtains, on this view, where natural equals are treated the same, and natural unequals are treated the same, i.e., receive an unequal portion of whatever social good is available, since unequals are only entitled to an unequal portion. That Aristotle's proportional equality, which is the basis for his theory of justice and the root idea of legal equality, is nonegalitarian (rejects equality among persons) is supported by multiple scholars (see, e.g., McKerlie 2001; Wolfsdorf 2017; Jiménez 2014).

Legal-equality-as-proportional-equality extends into Enlightenment political theory, particularly through the development of Social Contract Theory, the tradition of thought that addresses the problem of political authority by reference to an agreement between the citizens and the state. Social Contract Theory began in Europe in the seventeenth century within the context of an intellectual trend away from a teleological worldview and toward a mechanistic worldview in which the world worked in terms of causes and effects (Christman 2002). Despite the move away from teleology (that is, from metaphysics), social contract theorists nonetheless relied on the somewhat mystical concept of "natural rights" in their justifications for political authority.

One of the "natural rights" that belonged to all rational persons in virtue of being human, for the social contract theorists, was the right to equality. This is another way of saying that, for the social contract theorists, all persons were, at least theoretically, naturally equal. In pragmatic terms, what this meant was that one of the essential terms of the Social Contract was the guarantee of "equality before the law" (Johnson 2009).[9] While ideally this is a guarantee that everyone has an equal "natural" right to bring their disputes before an impartial sovereign and have their case heard impartially, in reality this was rarely how justice (or legal equality) was meted out.[10]

As was mentioned in the introduction, the Social Contract has been problematized by Charles Mills as obfuscating the ugly realities of group power and domination that mark the modern world and its theoretical underpinnings. Rather than a social contract between all members of a given modern society, the concept that marks modern societies is what Mills calls a "Racial Contract," understood as an agreement between and among nonracialized persons for the benefit of nonracialized persons. Rather than a society of equals, modern societies are built upon and rife with racial domination and exploitation.

The disconnect between Enlightenment ideals of freedom and equality and the reality of the central role of human chattel slavery and racial subjugation in the development and continuing operations of modern societies is evidence of the oddly hypocritical way in which modern societies operate. On the one hand, the modern (and contemporary) world is framed by an ideology of equal treatment under the law and "natural" rights and a rejection of the medieval focus on noble birth and the divine right of kings, but on the other hand, there is a routine and systematic relegation of an entire "race" of human beings to the status of natural slavery, natural inferiority, natural subjugation, and inferior social status. Aristotle refers to natural slaves as "tools" for the master of the house to do what he will in the management of his household, and his city-state. John Locke, the author of *Two Treatises of Government*, one of the key political writings of the modern age and in which Locke rejects slavery, also owned stock in slave trading companies and helped write the *Constitutions of Carolina* which explicitly provides for slavery (Farr 2008; Bernasconi 1992). Many of the writers of the founding documents of the United States owned slaves. Within this context, the proposition that the "all" in the idea that law should be applied impartially to all meant only nonracialized persons makes sense. There seems to be no other way to reconcile the ideology of Ancient and Enlightenment legal equality with the reality of the simultaneous relegation (in each case) of large swaths of the human family to an inferior, slave caste. Legal equality, along this line of reasoning, is only available to those who are equal. In the case of the contemporary United States, this arguably means nonracialized persons only. For similar reasons, legal equality arguably cannot address the problem of racial inequality in the United States. Applying the law impartially to all in the specific context in which whole segments of the population live in a constant state of social inequality, will necessarily lead to the perpetuation of the (unequal) racial status quo.

Nevertheless, the decisions of the Supreme Court since its 1978 decision in *Regents of the University of California v. Bakke* all utilize legal equality rather than social equality as the form of equality motivating decisions as to how to best interpret the Equal Protection Clause. As mentioned in chapter 2, the Court found in *Bakke* that unconstitutional reverse discrimination had occurred against a nonracialized applicant to a state medical school on the grounds that the school's special admissions program unconstitutionally used race in their hiring processes. This case marks the formalization, if not the outright invention, of the phenomenon of "reverse racism" as a constitutionally redressable injury. The invention of the concept of reverse racism is arguably wholly out of step with the goal of social/racial equality (as I have defined these terms), particularly in the present historical era.

Similarly, in *City of Richmond v. J.A. Croson Company* (1989), the Court found a violation against nonracialized persons in a Richmond set-aside program requiring construction companies who were awarded city contracts to award at least 30 percent of their subcontracts to minority-owned businesses (on the grounds that the plan denied nonracialized persons the opportunity to compete for the 30 percent based solely on their race). Moreover, in *Adarand Constructors, Inc. v. Peña* (1995), the Court found that all racial classifications must be analyzed under the same level of review (the extremely high level of strict scrutiny), and are presumptively unconstitutional unless they are narrowly tailored to meet a compelling governmental interest. This means effectively that racial classifications *per se* are presumptively unconstitutional, including, as was the case in *Adarand*, a policy of the U.S. Department of Transportation to give financial incentive to companies run by individuals who were members of historically disadvantaged minority groups. Moreover, in the 2003 cases of *Gratz v. Bollinger* and *Grutter v. Bollinger*, the Court found unconstitutional any school admission policy that renders an applicant's race the "defining feature of his or her application."

That the Court in its recent decisions interpreting the Equal Protection Clause is utilizing legal equality (equality in the abstract, which always amounts to equality for equals only and inequality for unequals) rather than social equality (equality of social status for racialized persons) is arguably self-evident and not in need of argument. The question is whether this is appropriate within the contemporary context in which the social inequality of racialized persons remains an obvious feature of modern American society.

Legal Equality Is Out of Step with the Purpose of the Clause

A look at the historical context of the Equal Protection Clause and the legislative history of the Fourteenth Amendment evidences that the purpose of the Clause was facilitation of the social equality of racialized persons, rather than their mere legal equality.

Historical Context

The Fourteenth Amendment was ratified in 1868, roughly two and a half years after the ratification of the Thirteenth Amendment, and about two years before ratification of the Fifteenth Amendment. Together these three Amendments are known as the Civil War Amendments. A bit of background about the historical time period is helpful. In early 1863, during the Civil War, President Lincoln, using his authority as commander in chief of the army, issued the Emancipation Proclamation, which freed all slaves living within the Confederacy (Franklin 1963).[11]

Later that year, Lincoln delivered the Gettysburg Address, a speech offered in dedication of the Soldiers' National Cemetery just four months after the Battle of Gettysburg where there had been a decisive, but bloody, Union victory (Sears 1920). Lincoln began the Gettysburg Address by reminding the crowd then present that just eighty-four years prior, in 1776, the United States had begun in dedication to the proposition that all men are created equal.[12] The Civil War ended in April of 1865 with the surrender of Confederate General Robert E. Lee (Rawley 1989). In December of that year, the Thirteenth Amendment, which banned slavery everywhere in the United States, was ratified. The Fourteenth Amendment (containing the Equal Protection Clause) was ratified in July 1868, and then the Fifteenth Amendment (prohibiting discrimination in voting "on account of race, color, or previous condition of servitude") was ratified in March of 1870.

Taken together, these various Civil War Amendments, and the facts surrounding their ratification, suggest that the central purpose for the inclusion of the Equal Protection Clause in the Fourteenth Amendment was to establish (especially to the southern states) that equal protection under the law for racialized Americans could and would be federally enforced.[13] Arguably, the reason the awesome power of the federal government of the United States was being used, through the ratification of the Civil War Amendments, to literally force the southern states to treat racialized Americans equally *was because the reality was that racialized Americans were clearly not being treated equally.* On a routine basis and on a systemic level, racialized Americans were being denied access to basic social goods like housing, jobs, income, and education. The Clause was included in the Fourteenth Amendment to address these inequities. In other words, the Equal Protection Clause was *remedial* in nature. It was placed in the Fourteenth Amendment to solve the very real problem of the widespread unequal access to basic social goods for racialized Americans, implemented through Jim Crow laws and social policies related thereto. It was in the face of the manifest and widespread, unequal access to basic social goods of racialized persons that the Equal Protection Clause was placed in the Fourteenth Amendment.[14]

Legislative History

As more evidence of this fact, the legislative history of the Fourteenth Amendment begins with a system of constitutional protection for the rights of free "Negroes and mulattoes" developed by a group known as the American Anti-Slavery Society during the years 1834 to 1835 (Graham 1968, 185). In the papers documenting the proceedings of this society, there is evidence of an "ingenious, exhaustive, and above all, prophetic constitutional attack on slavery" (Graham 1968, 168). These documents show that what had begun as an ethical and religious attack on slavery transmuted in this time period into a legal and constitutional attack (ibid., 169). Congressman Thaddeus Stevens, one of the ultimate sponsors of the Fourteenth Amendment, was an early member of this society (ibid.; Woodburn 1913/2017).

The legislative history of the Fourteenth Amendment continues with the Congressional debates that took place in 1866 during the 39th Congress. That history substantiates the conclusion that the Equal Protection Clause was meant to operate as a remedial measure to correct the widespread subjugation of racialized persons in America. The sponsors of the Fourteenth Amendment were Congressman Thaddeus Stevens and Senator Benjamin Wade (Schnapper 1985, 784). During the debates, Congressman Stevens made specific reference to the "all men are created equal" portion of Declaration of Independence, arguing that since this provision was already in the Declaration, the phraseology to this effect in the Fourteenth Amendment was clearly warranted. All that the Equal Protection Clause added, Stevens argued, was "to correct the unjust legislation of the States, so far that the law which operates upon one man shall operate *equally* on all" (Congressional Globe, 39th Congress, 1st Session 2459, 1866, italics in original).

That the primary purpose of the Fourteenth Amendment was to address the unequal status of racialized persons is further supported by the observation that the entire antislavery campaign—of which the Civil War Amendments were an undeniable outgrowth—was essentially a quest for enforcement of United States ideals that already existed but were being ignored, particularly in the former slave states (Graham 1968, 169). These ideals were that all U.S. citizens were entitled to the privileges and immunities of U.S. citizenship (per Article IV, Section 2 of the Constitution), that all citizens were entitled to due process of the law (per the Fifth Amendment), and that all persons were created equal (per the Declaration of Independence).

While there were several writers of the larger Fourteenth Amendment, Section 1 (which includes the Equal Protection Clause) was written by Representative John Bingham of Ohio (Stephens and Sheb 2008, 18). The writers of the larger Fourteenth Amendment consisted of two different factions of the Republican party of the day (Trefousse 1969). One faction consisted of avid abolitionists, known as the Radicals, who were motivated to support the Civil War by a desire to end slavery and to provide racialized persons with the same federal rights, privileges, and protections as other Americans (ibid.). The other faction consisted of persons who were at best indifferent to the abolition of slavery and the rights of racialized persons, and had been motivated to support the war by a desire to preserve the union (ibid.).

Representative Bingham was a Radical. The Radicals had been committed to the abolition of slavery and to equal treatment for former slaves since at least 1863 when President Lincoln had signed the Emancipation Proclamation, and many of them had been committed to the cause well before that (Trefousse 1969). At least since the *Dred Scott* decision of 1857—in which the Supreme Court held that racialized persons were not citizens of the United States and could never be citizens owing to the fact that the Framers of the United States had considered racialized persons to be "beings of an inferior order" with "no rights which the white man was bound to respect" *Dred Scott v. Sanford* (1857)—the Radicals had been driven to amend the Constitution to clarify that, in their view, the *Dred Scott* decision was wrongly decided (Schwartz 1973, 19).

Between 1856 and 1859, Representative Bingham made three major speeches in Congress relevant to his views on the meaning of the Fourteenth Amendment (Graham 1968, 161, citing Cong. Globe., 34th Congress, 1st Session Appendix 124 [1856]; Cong. Globe, 34th Congress, 3rd Session Appendix 135–40 [1857]; and Cong. Globe, 35th Congress, 2nd Session 981–85 [1859]). All three speeches focused on due process rights. In the second speech, he stressed that the "absolute equality of all and the equal protection of each" are "American constitutional ideals," noting that the Constitution makes no distinction on the basis of either "complexion or birth" (Graham 1968, 57). In the third speech Bingham used the concepts of "natural and inherent rights," "sacred rights . . . as universal and indestructible as the human race," and "equality of natural rights" to seek constitutional sanction for his antislavery views (ibid.). Graham tied these "natural" rights to the Constitution by highlighting that the Fifth Amendment uses the word "person" instead of "citizen" (ibid.). Bingham also made sure that a guarantee of equal protection of the laws was included in every single draft of Section 1 (James 1966). Although Bingham utilized the fraught language of "natural" rights in his speeches, his purpose, given the context, is clear: to emphasize that racialized persons were human beings, and as such, were entitled to be members of the society of equals to which the founding documents of the United States ostensibly ascribed.

Legal Equality Is Out of Step with the Contemporary Sociocultural Context

It seems fairly indisputable that in the contemporary era, the legal and social equality of racialized persons has improved since 1868, the year the Fourteenth Amendment was ratified. This improvement of condition has led some commentators to suggest that, even if it can be fairly said that the original intent of the Equal Protection Clause was to provide a way for recently freed racialized persons to achieve social equality in America, this remedial purpose is of little contemporary significance in terms of how the Equal Protection Clause should be understood and applied today (see, e.g., Glazer 1975, Bickel 1955).[15] Since the pressing problem of severe inequality between racialized and nonracialized persons in America that was attendant to the social context in which the Equal Protection Clause was created is no longer as acute, these commentators suggest, understanding the Equal Protection Clause as a remedial instrument for improving the social equality of racialized persons is simply outdated. Other conservative commentators—often the same jurists who advocate originalism—argue simply that the Equal Protection Clause was never intended to specially protect racialized persons, usually citing the text itself (containing no specific reference to racialized persons) as evidence.[16]

But, the vast majority of responsible scholarship on this point takes the position that the equality status of racialized persons as a group has not, on close examination, improved as much as one might have hoped since 1868, particularly in the areas of income, net worth, and education (Lawson 1992; Waller 2001; Hilfiker 2003). While there is little doubt that there has been improvement since 1868 regarding the legal and social equality of racialized persons, this is not saying much on the question of the equality status of racialized persons today, given that the point of reference for racialized persons as a group was that in 1868 racialized persons were widely considered to be patently, manifestly, biologically, irrevocably, morally, intellectually, and physically inferior to nonracialized persons (Hoffman 1896/2004; Finkelman 2003; Finkleman 2001; Griffin 2000; Darwin and Ridley 1996; Shipman 1994; Davies 1955; Stanton 1960; Fredrickson 1971/2008; Gould 1981/1996; Irvine 1955; Jordan 1968/2012; Lovejoy 1942). This view of racialized persons was so prevalent in the post–Civil War era, in fact, that widespread attempts were made—through, for example, the enactment of Jim Crow laws all over the

South—to keep racialized persons physically separated from nonracialized persons in any and all public contexts in which the two groups might come into social contact (Takaki 1990; Woodward 1967/2006; Kluger 1975; Packard 2002; Thomas 1997). The significance of this almost unimaginable and horrific state of affairs cannot be overstated; for, in effect, racialized persons were the social lepers of the mid- to late nineteenth-century social scene in America, and this was particularly the case in the former slave states.[17]

So, while it is true that certainly, there was no place to go but up from a social status similar to that of lepers, the reality of the social condition of racialized persons in America today is that it is still dire and quite unequal to that of nonracialized persons on all frontiers (Oliver and Shapiro 1995/2006; Squires 1994; Brenner and Spayd 1993; Dedman 1988; Feagin and Parker 1990; Feagin and Sikes 1994; Oliver 1980; Collins et al. 2004). There are still dramatic gaps between nonracialized persons and racialized persons in income, wealth, housing, education, and occupation (ibid., Bonilla-Silva 2010, 209)[18] and the overwhelming majority of responsible analysts agree that the persistence of racial inequality today is due, to a very significant extent, to the persistence and continuing significance of racism and racial discrimination rooted in the perceived status inequality of racialized persons (ibid., Feagin 1991, Bell 1992b).[19] Moreover, and from the perspective of a substantial number of contemporary critical race theorists, the explanation for the continuing existence of racial discrimination in America can in turn be most responsibly traced to the unique way in which the concept of blackness (human "racial" blackness) became indelibly associated with social inferiority in America through the creation and perpetuation of the institution of chattel slavery, and the government's endorsement of that institution (however explicit or tacit) from the very beginning of the country's creation (Mills 1997; Gotanda 1995; Harris 1993; Bell 1992a; Matsuda 1995; Williams 1995).[20] Thus, in the contemporary era, it is far more than fair to say that the social status of racialized persons in America is still quite unequal, and as a result, racialized persons as a group are still in need of the kind of special protection that the Equal Protection Clause was designed to provide.

Some argue, however, that the switch in focus from social equality to legal equality on the part of the Supreme Court is warranted, owing to the fact that slavery was abolished over a hundred and fifty years ago, such that the continuing unequal social status of racialized persons in the United States is attributable more to "cultural differences" between racialized persons and nonracialized persons than to the vestiges of slavery. Arguments such as these usually rest on the claim that government-sponsored discrimination (e.g., de jure segregation) no longer exists, and has not existed for some time. If this is true, the argument goes, the government has no responsibility to address or remedy the continuing social inequality between racialized and nonracialized persons. In other words, if the cause for continuing status inequality is racialized persons themselves and not state action, it is not the responsibility of the government to provide a remedy for it. Leaving aside for the sake of argument the question of whether anyone (racialized or nonracialized) would intentionally behave in such a way as to facilitate their own unequal status in society, it is not necessary to investigate the question of whether racialized persons themselves (or the "culture" of racialized persons) are contributing to their continued inequality along racial lines in the United States since there is sufficient research showing that the social inequality of racialized persons has always been and continues to this day to be deliberately and intentionally generated by the actions of nonracialized persons in positions of institutional power, such that any contributions made by racialized persons themselves to their own inequality is negligible by comparison.

Richard Rothstein makes the case for this claim in his recent, *The Color of Law: A Forgotten History of How Our Government Segregated America* (2017). There, Rothstein shows that at least as regards racial segregation in housing, the social inequality of racialized persons that continues to this day all over the United States—but particularly in places like Ferguson, Baltimore, Milwaukee, and Charlotte—is not the product of what we call dismissively "de facto segregation," or self-imposed racial segregation, but instead is a product of racially explicit and intentional policies of federal, state, and local governments who, for many, many years defined where racialized and nonracialized persons should and would live. Rothstein powerfully writes,

> Today's residential segregation in the North, South, Midwest and West is not the unintended consequences of individual choices and of otherwise well-meaning law or regulation but *of unhidden public policy that explicitly segregated every metropolitan area in the United States.* The policy was so systematic and forceful that its effects endure to the present time. Without our government's purposeful imposition of racial segregation, the other causes [of social inequality]—private prejudice, white flight, real estate steering, bank redlining, income differences, and self-segregation—still would have existed but with far less opportunity for expression. Segregation by intentional government action is not *de facto*. Rather, it is what courts call *de jure*: segregation by law and policy (Rothstein 2017, vii–viii; emphasis added).

Rothstein continues, "The stereotypes and attitudes that support racial discrimination have their roots in the system of slavery *upon which the nation was founded*. So to most of us, it should now seem reasonable to agree that Congress was correct when it determined that prohibiting African Americans from buying or renting decent housing perpetuated second-class citizenship that was a relic of slavery" (ix). Pointedly, Rothstein concludes that although there is no *judicial* remedy for a policy that the Supreme Court wrongheadedly approves (like inventing so-called reverse discrimination), it does not follow that there is no remedy available. "It is up to the people," Rothstein stresses, "through our elected representatives, to enforce our Constitution by implementing the remedy" (xi). "By failing to recognize that *we now live with the severe, enduring effects of de jure segregation, we avoid confronting our constitutional obligation to reverse it*," Rothstein concludes (xi; emphasis added).

To understand the necessity for a change in the way the Supreme Court interprets the Equal Protection Clause, then, is to first admit that it was our government who created the social inequality now faced by racialized persons in the United States through policies and practices from which our country has still not recovered. The institution of chattel slavery is certainly one of those pieces, as are the Jim Crow laws enacted all over the country after the end of the Civil War. Governmentally sponsored and enforced de jure segregation in housing is certainly one of those pieces as well, as Rothstein artfully shows.

Legal Equality Facilitates and Perpetuates the Problem of Racial Inequality

As mentioned above, one of the ways to characterize legal equality in the context of equal protection jurisprudence and racial discrimination is that it is manifested in the concept of the color-blind principle. Recall that the color-blind principle, generally speaking, is the idea that it is unconstitutional to ever distinguish between persons on the basis of race. However, numerous critical race theorists take issue with the idea that racial categorization is always unconstitutional. For example, Neil Gotanda has observed that the color-blind principle (what he calls "color blind constitutionalism") "fosters white racial domination" (Gotanda 1995, 257). Gotanda continues, "A color-blind interpretation of the Constitution legitimates and thereby maintains the social, economic, and political advantages that whites hold over other Americans" (ibid.). When race is characterized as objective and apolitical, Gotanda continues, as the Court has done in recent equal protection law, the context-dependent and mutable nature of racial identity is obfuscated and the history of how races and racial hierarchy were created in the United States (particularly the "black" race as a low-status race), that is, in order to justify the enslavement of human persons in the antebellum period, becomes disguised and discounted. *Plessy v. Ferguson* (1896)—the famous case that legalized Separate But Equal Doctrine—for Gotanda, typifies how this process works. In upholding a Louisiana statute requiring separate seating for racialized and nonracialized persons in public carriers, the Court turned a blind eye to history, maintaining that the statute segregating racialized from nonracialized persons "said nothing about the status of blacks," holding instead that the statute was racially neutral (Gotanda 1995, 263). The extraction from social context and history of race-conscious laws, for Gotanda, distorts the entire legal enterprise, leaving equal protection law powerless to do the work it was intended to do. Disturbingly, for Gotanda, "[c]olor-blindness strikes down Jim Crow segregation but offers no vision for attacking less overt forms of racial subordination" (Gotanda 1995, 269). In the absence of a clear vision for attacking nonovert racial subordination, the laws become available for exploitation by forces that operate in the service of racial subordination. What we need instead of color-blind constitutionalism, for Gotanda, is a constitutional jurisprudence on race that supports efforts to address white privilege. "Because of a genuine concern that any change in doctrine may weaken the struggle against racial oppression," however, according to Gotanda, "the [Court] must maintain all existing constitutional protection for racial minorities against a resurgence of the white supremacist movement," Gotanda compellingly writes (272).

Critical race theorist Robin West divides the various interpretations of the Equal Protection Clause offered by the Supreme Court from 1868 to 1989 into two main categories: (1) a "formal" meaning, and (2) a "substantive" meaning (West 1990). The formal meaning of the Clause is that "legislators must treat like groups alike, and the laws they make must reflect this mandate by being "rational" (ibid.).[21] So, if two groups are similar in a way that is legally pertinent, the law may not treat them differently. Any distinction between groups of persons in a given law, on this view, must be rationally related to pre-existing differences between the groups toward a rational (code for legitimate) end. A law that fails this test has failed to provide equal protection of the law. By contrast, the substantive meaning of the Clause is that "legislators must use law to ensure that no social group, such as nonracialized persons or men, wrongfully subordinates another social group, such as racialized persons or women" (ibid.). So, if one group dominates another group, then the legislature should take steps to end the domination. If a state fails to take such steps, the subordinated group has been denied equal protection of the law.

According to the formal meaning of the Clause, any state differentiation between nonracialized persons and racialized persons is prima facie irrational, since the two groups are "alike" for legal purposes and therefore should be treated alike. Race itself, on this view, cannot, alone, justify differential treatment. Accordingly, race-conscious policies are unconstitutional without proof positive of identifiable past discrimination against racialized persons that can be shown to have clearly caused a difference between the two groups, such that differential treatment is now justified to correct that. Contrast this with the substantive meaning of the Clause, according to which race-conscious policies are certainly permissible and perhaps mandatory. Along this train of thought, nonracialized persons are dominant in society and racialized persons are subordinate, such that the Equal Protection Clause requires positive steps to equalize the two.

Accordingly, as has been mentioned earlier in this text, utilization of formal or legal equality, or the impartial application of the law to all people, necessarily results in the perpetuation of inequality based on race since American society is teeming with racial inequality, defined as social inequality based on race.

CONCLUDING REFLECTIONS

The commonality between legal equality (understood as rooted in Aristotle's proportional equality) and the ideology of American chattel slavery is clear, and the reverberations for the equality status of racialized persons are also clear, playing out in the spate of recent successful equal protection cases where "reverse racism" is alleged and found to have occurred. Since racialized persons are *biologically* black (borrowing a line of reasoning from chapter 2), current equal protection reasoning seems to go, they are *naturally* unequal, rather than unequal as a result of the legacy of chattel slavery. Legal equality is the goal of equal protection law, on this view, not social equality; and equal protection law is available to protect only the equality of those naturally deserving of equality (e.g., biological "whites") rather than as a remedy to correct the social inequality forcibly imposed upon racialized persons by the sociohistorical phenomenon of American chattel slavery, Jim Crow laws, the state-sponsored segregation of housing along racial lines, and the aftermath of all of these phenomena.

NOTES

1. This is not to say I will never deviate from these four concepts of equality. It is just to say I will use these four concepts as points of reference to begin the investigation.

2. With an exception here and there where I felt it was important to engage a particular egalitarian scholar, in this work I have not explicitly engaged the philosophical scholarship surrounding egalitarianism as a political theory or ideal for the reasons that egalitarianism is multifaceted and complex, with each strand prioritizing one or more of the different forms of equality as David Johnston has defined them in different ways, including defining equality in terms of different conditions such as (1) equality of what (e.g., opportunity or outcome), (2) equality of whom, and (3) whether equality is valuable per se or has instrumental value only. Moreover, for purposes of the current project, Johnston's four types of equality sufficiently capture the relevant variations.

3. For many years, scholars across disciplines have been remarking on the strange way equal protection law has developed and changed. Virtually all agree that there has been a change in equal protection law (at least vis-à-vis how racial discrimination should be handled), but different scholars have characterized the change differently. Many characterize the change as a move from a "color-conscious" approach to a "color-blind" approach (see, e.g., Kull 1992). Others characterize the change as moving from a focus on "anti-subordination" to "anti-classification" (see, e.g., Fiss 1976 and Balkin and Siegel 2003–2004). The anti-subordination principle is also known as the

antisubjugation principle, the equal citizenship principle, and the anticaste principle (see, e.g., Karst 1989, Mackinnon 1987/1994, and Tribe 1988).

4. Anderson's critique of luck egalitarianism (on the grounds that it fails to prioritize equal concern and respect for all citizens in that it creates stigmatizing or marginalizing hierarchies of worth) contains a similar line of reasoning (see Anderson 1999).

5. Notably, this is virtually the exact same position on racial identity that I recommend the Supreme Court adopt.

6. The idea here, of course, is that state remediation for racial inequality is only in order to the extent that it was generated by the state. This is an idea that is consistent with the arguments made in this book. The *reason* equal protection law should be at the disposal of racialized persons but not nonracialized persons, the argument in this book goes, is that the state created the racial inequality that the Equal Protection Clause was designed to remedy.

7. See Fourie 2011 and Mills 2015.

8. I will say more on the relationship between this concept (that racial inequality hurts nonracialized persons as much as racialized persons) and Critical Race Theory's idea of "interest convergence" in chapter 6.

9. See, for example, Hobbes 1651, 184: "The safety of the People requireth further, from him or them that have the Sovereign Power, that Justice be equally administered to all degrees of People; that is, that as well thee rich and mighty, as poor and obscure persons, may be righted of the injuries done them."

10. For example, the Separate But Equal Doctrine inaugurated by *Plessy v. Ferguson* (1896), according to which separate accommodations for racialized and nonracialized persons on a public train were deemed "equal," was understood to accomplish legal equality, since everyone (the racialized and nonracialized alike) could use the train for transportation.

11. The Emancipation Proclamation did not free slaves living in the loyal slave states of Maryland, Kentucky, Delaware, and Missouri, nor slaves living in certain parts of Virginia and Louisiana that were controlled by the United States. Lincoln had used his authority as commander in chief of the army to free slaves through the Emancipation Proclamation, and so could only free the slaves held by those in rebellion against the United States (Franklin 1963).

12. A clear reference to the Declaration of Independence.

13. Citing *The Slaughterhouse Cases* (1873), historian Howard Jay Graham has stated that the Civil War Amendments were all framed on behalf of racialized persons ("the slave race"). "This, of course, is especially true of the Fourteenth Amendment" (Graham 1968, 157). In fact, for Graham, it is "patently absurd to deny the antislavery origins of the [Fourteenth Amendment]" (ibid., 161).

14. Constitutional historians strongly agree among themselves that the Fourteenth Amendment had its origins in the antislavery movement (Baer 1983, 57).

15. The Center for Individual Rights ("CIR"), a strong proponent of this view, is a law firm whose primary activity is to challenge race-conscious programs on the basis that they infringe upon "individual rights." The CIR was counsel for the petitioner in both of the Michigan cases.

16. This view is of course in complete disregard for the Congressional debates surrounding the enactment of the Fourteenth Amendment and in complete disregard for the sociohistorical context of the text, i.e., in the aftermath of slavery and in conjunction with two other Amendments (the Thirteenth and Fifteenth), both of which are prima facie directed at the rights of racialized persons.

17. The effect on the collective American psyche of the widespread and legally enforced mark of social inferiority placed on black people by slavery and the Jim Crow laws that followed after slavery is the cornerstone of what Bill Lawson and others have called the "racial consciousness" of contemporary American society (see, e.g., Lawson 1995; Banton 1988). For "racial realists" like Derrick Bell, racism must be understood as a permanent feature of American society owing to the indelible effect that slavery and Jim Crow laws have had on the subconscious mind-set of every

American (Bell 1992b). For these thinkers, no responsible analysis of the state of black people today and/or a suggestion of what do about it can take place unless this fact of life in America is first soberly taken into account. I compare the social stigma attached to being black in America to the traditional stigma against leprosy because of the enforced social separation experienced by both groups (by racialized persons during the Jim Crow era and by lepers since the Middle Ages). On the enforced social isolation of lepers, see, for example, W. H. Jopling, 1991.

18. See Amaad Rivera, Jeannette Huezo, Christina Kasica, and Dedrick Muhammad. 2009. "State of the Dream 2009: The Silent Depression." Boston: United for a Fair Economy, for a detailed report on the severity of income, wealth, housing, educational, and occupation inequality between nonracialized persons and racialized persons in 2009.

19. This is true despite the popularity of works like Charles Murray's *Losing Ground* (1984/2015), Murray and Herrnstein's *The Bell Curve: Intelligence and Class Structure in American Life* (1996), and Abigail and Stephan Thernstrom's *America in Black and White* (1997), in which the continuing inequality between nonracialized persons and racialized persons in America is attributed to the presumed cultural, moral, ethical, intellectual, or family "deficiencies" of racialized persons.

20. Several theorists have observed that the uniquely American institution of chattel slavery, that contained three elements that other forms of slavery have not contained, i.e., (1) the association of slave status with a certain set of phenotypical physical traits (i.e., what are commonly understood to be "black" phenotypical traits), (2) the idea that slave status was hereditary, and (3) the idea that the slaves themselves were a form of property associated with the real estate on which they worked like buildings or livestock, together created in the American psyche a kind of ineradicable association between phenotypical physical traits associated with being from the African continent and inferior social or legal status. The question of the degree to which the American institution of chattel slavery was, in fact, endorsed by the federal government from the beginning is a contested question. However, there is much scholarship supporting the view that the original constitution itself (the main body to the exclusion of the Amendments) contains several provisions meant to accommodate those among the Framers who were slaveholders (Mills 1997). The constitutional provisions most often cited as supporting slavery are Article I, Section 2, Paragraph 3; Article I, Section 8, Paragraph 15; Article I, Section 9, Paragraph 1, and Article IV, Section 2, Paragraph 3.

21. See also Tussman and TenBroeke, 1949.

FIVE

The Special Case of Multiracial Racialized Persons

Oddly,[1] there are currently no U.S. laws or court decisions specifically protecting *multiracial* racialized persons from racial discrimination (Williams 2006; Daniel 2002).[2] In fact, multiracial racialized Americans have been long left out of the antidiscrimination law loop as a result of their status as belonging simultaneously to multiple legally established racial groups and to no one legally established racial group in particular. This state of affairs is a problem for multiracial racialized Americans because in order to bring a claim of racial discrimination, a prospective antidiscrimination plaintiff must identify as belonging to at least one and to only one legally established racial group.[3]

In the early years of antidiscrimination law, a person raising a claim of unconstitutional racial discrimination had to be a member of a particular monoracial minority group with a history of having been discriminated against. In constitutional parlance, the plaintiff first had to identify as being a member of a "suspect class." "Suspect class" has many definitions in the case law. One definition is a group of people with a history of having been discriminated against in America. Another way of defining a "suspect class" is as a "discrete and insular minority group." Yet another way is as a group that is politically powerless. Still another way is as a group in possession of an "immutable characteristic" on the basis of which discrimination would be unfair in a particular context. In practice, this meant one had to be a member of a monoracial minority group or ethnic group with a history of having been discriminated against in America (Asian, Latino/a, Black, or Native American). If this requirement was met, the law or policy in question would be subject to a very strict level of judicial review, and the result would likely be that the law or policy in question would be struck down as unconstitutional.

Today, the barrier for multiracial racialized plaintiffs is different. In the present day, while the barrier of belonging to multiple legally established racial groups remains a problem, the new, practical barrier for multiracial racialized plaintiffs in antidiscrimination cases is that they belong to *no particular* racial group. This is a barrier because over the years, the threshold requirement for initiating a legally recognizable case of racial discrimination moved from requiring the plaintiff to identify as a member of a "suspect class" to requiring that the law or policy in question involve a "suspect classification." Between the 1938 case of *United States v. Carolene Products* (in which the Supreme Court first mentions that prejudice against "discrete and insular minorities" may be a special condition requiring closer judicial scrutiny of laws affecting such groups) and the 1978 case of *Regents of the University of California v. Bakke* (in which the Supreme Court held that racial classifications per se are racially discriminatory), the Supreme Court decided a series of cases (including, for example, the 1944 case of *Korematsu v. United States* where the Court held, in the midst of the Japanese internment controversy, that classifications based on nationality were inherently suspect) in which the court gradually shifted focus in antidiscrimination cases from protecting particular, historically oppressed groups to protecting everyone from racial discrimination per se.

Race and ethnicity are the prototypical suspect classifications. What this means is that, currently, if a law or policy discriminates between people on the basis of race or ethnicity, the law is subject to a much higher level of judicial scrutiny than it otherwise would be. As antidiscrimination law is presently treated by the courts, in other words, people of *any* legally established racial or ethnic group (including nonracialized persons) can bring a claim of discrimination.

While the distinction between "suspect class" analysis (based on the idea that members of "suspect classes" are the intended beneficiaries of antidiscrimination law) and "suspect classification" analysis (based on the idea that racial classifications per se are the intended targets of antidiscrimination law) is not altogether clear in the case law, one thing that is consistent across the board is that a prospective antidiscrimination plaintiff must first identify as a member of a single racial group before bringing an antidiscrimination claim. Judicial decisions regarding the right of people who identify as multiracial to equal protection of the laws or their rights under employment discrimination laws are always muddled and internally inconsistent, with the relevant judicial decisions often switching back and forth between recognizing the multiracial racialized person as first a member of one race and then another, but never both or all; that is, never recognizing the multiracial racialized person as a multiracial person. Multiracial racialized persons and the law have highlighted, however, that multiracial racialized persons very likely qualify as a "suspect class." Some of the factors cited in support of this claim are that multiracial racialized persons have experienced a history of discrimination based on the "immutable characteristic" of being mixed race, are a "discrete and insular" minority group in virtue of facing discrimination based on their status as multiracial racialized persons, and are excluded from the political process in the sense that their racial status is not acknowledged as legitimate. In other words, multiracial racialized persons, as multiracial racialized persons, have been the subject of much racial hostility in the United States, as well as structural alienation from the benefits of mainstream antidiscrimination law.

Whether multiracial racialized persons are a suspect class or not, however, race still remains a suspect *classification* under current antidiscrimination law theory. But, since multiracial racialized persons are not understood as a legally established racial group, in order to benefit from antidiscrimination law, the multiracial plaintiff is faced with a troubling problem: either identify exclusively as a member of one racial minority group or go without redress. This problem is troubling for at least two reasons. First, since multiracial racialized persons face discrimination *as* multiracial racialized persons and not as members of a given monoracial minority group, the remedies currently offered by the law are not adequately tailored to the wrong suffered. Second, persons who identify as multiracial are required to legally suppress their multiracial identity for the sake of being able to avail themselves of equal protection of the laws. As a result of these factors, many potential multiracial plaintiffs opt to suffer discrimination in silence rather than be forced to mischaracterize the discrimination they suffer in ways that suppress their racial identity.

In this chapter, I will (1) provide an overview of the historical engagement between multiracial racialized persons and the law; (2) identify and examine factors contributing to the failure of current antidiscrimination laws to protect multiracial racialized Americans from racial discrimination; (3) argue in favor of a distinctive group identity for multiracial racialized Americans, with particular emphasis placed on the need for a distinctive group identity within the framework of antidiscrimination law; and (4) suggest an additional modification to antidiscrimination law (i.e., the utilization of sociohistorical race) in order to better protect multiracial racialized Americans from racial discrimination.

HISTORICAL ENGAGEMENT BETWEEN MULTIRACIAL RACIALIZED PERSONS AND THE LAW

Antimiscegenation Laws

Antipathy toward race mixing is a fact of U.S. history, typified in the over three hundred years of antimiscegenation laws that began in the early British colonies in North America and continued later in the United

States. In colonial America, criminal sanction for those marrying or cohabitating across racial lines was common, beginning in the second half of the seventeenth century (Wadlington 1996). The words "miscegenation"—Latin for "to mix types" or "to mix families" from the words "miscere" (to mix) and "genus" (type, family, or descent)—and "mulatto"—from the Latin "mūlus" meaning "mule" or the hybrid offspring of a horse and a donkey—became commonly used during the colonial period (ibid.). Virginia and Maryland were the first colonies to enact anti-miscegenation statutes, in 1662 and 1663 respectively. Over the life of anti-miscegenation laws—roughly from the mid-seventeenth century through the Supreme Court's decision in *Loving v. Virginia* in 1967, punishments for violating anti-miscegenation laws varied from state to state, ranging from a "sound whipping" (for a nonracialized man who was caught "lying with a negro" in Virginia in 1630 [ibid.]) to up to five years of prison with hard labor (see *State v. Brown*, 108 S.E.2d 233, 234 [La. 1959]). Rationales offered in support of these laws often centered on society's interest in keeping the races pure. At the root of these rationales was the idea that members of racial minority groups were physically, mentally, and morally inferior to members of the majority nonracialized group, so the nonracialized race was thought to be corrupted, soiled, and degraded by "mixing" with the racialized one.

The general understanding of race in popular American culture, in other words, included the notion that races were both biologically based and pure, necessitating antimiscegeneation laws in order to stop the impurity from spreading. The myth of racial purity continued into the twentieth century, and continues to exist today in the minds of most Americans, despite evidence available at least as early as Darwin that all members of the human species have a common African genesis (see Darwin 1871/2008; Larson 2006), and therefore that there really were no pure human races. The eugenics movement of the late nineteenth and early twentieth centuries supported the erroneous claim that there were such things as pure human races, with the result that the criminalization of marriage or cohabitation (and ultimately, procreation) between members of different races seemed justified for the good of so-called "racial progress."

Jim Crow Laws and Segregation

One of the most fascinating turns in the history of multiracial racialized persons and antidiscrimination law is the case of *Plessy v. Ferguson.* This case gave constitutional blessing to racial discrimination in public accommodations and augured in the Jim Crow era. Throughout the case, the court makes reference to "the two races," as if, in the first place, there are races, and in the second place, there are only two ("black" and "white"). In the court's mind, a clear line of demarcation existed between "the two races," in terms of the ability of members of the black race to freely associate with members of the nonracialized race, even though there was some argument in the states as to how one might draw the line or even on how to distinguish one race from the other. The court itself pointed out, "It is true that the question of the proportion of colored blood necessary to constitute a colored person, as distinguished from a white person, is one upon which there is a difference of opinion in the different states." In support of its decision in *Plessy*, the Supreme Court cited the then constitutionality of state bans on "intermarriage" and state laws requiring racial segregation in public schools, arguing that it had repeatedly (and presumably, justifiably) made "the distinction between laws interfering with the political equality of the Negro and those requiring the separation of the two races."

The effect of *Plessy* was official federal support for the idea that there were races in the world, that these races were distinguishable, and that these races could be legally segregated. The result was approximately sixty-five years of official, federally sanctioned separation of members of monoracial minority groups from nonracialized persons in all sorts of public accommodations. The existence of multiracial racialized persons in the United States problematized this framework. Did they belong in the nonracialized section of public accommodations or the black? The emergence of what became known as the "one-drop rule" offered a solution to that problem.

The "One-Drop" Rule

While early American courts relied on one or more of three traditional rules to determine a person's race (physical appearance, blood fraction, or association); between 1830 and 1840, northern American courts began to use what became known as the "one-drop" rule instead (Sweet 2005; Davis 1991; Daniel 2002; Jordan 2014; Spickard 1989). According to this rule, anyone with any known black ancestry was categorized as black. The one-drop rule then spread slowly southward and became the unwritten law throughout the United States by the turn of the twentieth century (ibid.). The pervasiveness of the one-drop rule lent popular support in America to what is known as "hypodescent," according to which persons of multiracial ancestry are identified as belonging to the racialized group aspect of their ancestry (Brunsma and Rockquemore, 2002). Within a culture that accepts the one-drop rule and hypodescent as authoritative on the question of racial identity, multiracial identity is rendered nonsensical, and therefore legally unrecognizable.

Therefore, the history of the engagement between multiracial racialized persons and antidiscrimination law in America is one in which the status of multiracial racialized persons *as multiracial* has either been systematically ignored or obliterated.

THE FAILURE OF ANTIDISCRIMINATION LAWS TO PROTECT MULTIRACIAL RACIALIZED PERSONS

There are several current factors contributing to the nonrecognition in U.S. law of multiracial racialized persons as a legally established group for antidiscrimination law purposes. These include the persistence of the mistaken belief that race is rooted in biology and science and the current failure of antidiscrimination law to acknowledge that the illegality, wrong, and harm of racial discrimination is that it perpetuates historically situated, institutionalized racial oppression.

Biological Races

Notions about race in the United States are fraught with confusion. To help clarify this confusion, it is helpful to distinguish at least three ways in which the phenomenon of human racial categories can be understood: (1) according to colloquial understanding, (2) according to scientific understanding, and (3) according to sociological understanding. The colloquial understanding defines race in one or more of the following ways: as being based in biology; as having a genetic basis; as involving common ancestry or descent; as based on shared external physical characteristics (sometimes called phenotype); or as involving the presumption of a correlation between shared external physical characteristics and more internal traits such as intellectual or moral features. The scientific understanding rejects all aspects of the colloquial understanding. For some time, there has been widespread, although not undisputed, acceptance in the scientific community of the fact that the phenomenon of human racial categories has no biological or genetic basis (Montagu 1942; UNESCO 1951; Livingstone 1962, Lewontin 1972; Hubbard 1999, and Graves 2001) and, therefore, no link between any biological, physical, or genetic trait and any internal features. The sociological understanding accepts the scientific understanding but adds the fact that American culture still operates as if race exists (in the biological sense). In this sociological understanding, race is sometimes referred to as having a sociocultural or sociohistorical existence. The upshot of American confusion over race is that although science has clearly shown that there are no biological or genetically based human races, American culture still operates as if there were.

Even more troubling is the inclusion of beliefs in racial purity and racial essentialism in the biological concept of race that prevails in American culture. According to this perspective, there are biological races in the world that are identifiable in terms of biological traits. These biological races are "pure" and can be easily differentiated from one another in terms of objective, observable phenomena. There are certain nonphysical traits associated with these pure races as well, such as intellectual capacity, moral sensibility, and aesthetic tastes (in music, in art, etc.).

Multiracial racialized persons throw this picture of race into havoc. It does not make sense if they exist. In order to have rights (including rights against racial discrimination) as multiracial racialized persons, multiracial racialized persons must first be real. If biological race adequately describes race, then multiracial racialized persons are not real and do not exist.

Racial Discrimination Perpetuates Historically Situated Oppression

Antidiscrimination law was designed for the purpose of remedying racial discrimination against historically marginalized and oppressed groups rather than to remedy racial discrimination *per se* (Botts 2013). Equal protection law originated with the ratification of the Fourteenth Amendment to the U.S. Constitution in 1868. The Fourteenth Amendment included the Equal Protection Clause, which says, "No state shall . . . deny to any person within its jurisdiction the equal protection of the laws" (U.S. Const. amend. XIV § 1). The historical context in which the Equal Protection Clause was created provides insight as to its meaning, purpose, and goals. The Fourteenth Amendment is one of a set of constitutional amendments enacted shortly after the Civil War ended in April of 1865 (Rawley 1989). The legislative history of the Fourteenth Amendment, much of which is found in the debates that took place in 1866 during the 39th Congress, supports the interpretation that the Equal Protection Clause was meant to operate as a remedial measure to correct the widespread subjugation of racialized persons as a group in America.

Similarly, employment discrimination law was enacted to overturn the reality that for the first 350 years of American history, the best of everything was reserved for nonracialized men (Gold 2001). It was enacted to increase the likelihood that persons other than nonracialized males would benefit from meritorious hiring decisions. Employment discrimination law is rooted in the Unemployment Relief Act of 1933, which stated, "In employing citizens for the purpose of this Act no discrimination shall be made on account of race, color, or creed" (Jasper 2008). Title VII of the Civil Rights Act of 1964 ("Title VII") evolved out of the Unemployment Relief Act and serves as the basis for employment discrimination cases today. Title VII prohibits discrimination on the basis of race, color, religion, sex, or national origin and was passed primarily to protect women and racialized persons from discrimination (ibid.).

Title VII was designed as a guide to the litigation of employment discrimination cases and therefore goes into great detail about the kinds of behaviors that constitute illegal discrimination (e.g., harassment), the kinds of behaviors that are protected (e.g., opposition or reporting discrimination to the employer), the kinds of employers covered, and the kinds of bases for discrimination covered by the Act (e.g., race and sex). There is no evidence in the Act itself or in the legislative history surrounding the Act that its purpose was to promote racial understanding, eliminate racism, or eliminate racial discrimination. Nor is there evidence that by "race" or "protected class" the Act meant biological race. Instead, history reveals that Title VII was enacted during the height of the civil rights movement and was designed to allow plaintiffs facing employment discrimination on the basis of being members of historically oppressed groups a legal remedy for that discrimination.

Despite all of the above, antidiscrimination law operates as if the wrong to be remedied by this area of law is treating the race of a person as significant in situations in which it should not be so treated. In other words, the historical context of antidiscrimination law has been forgotten in favor of treating racial discrimination as if it occurs in a vacuum, as if it, in itself, is the problem to be addressed by antidiscrimination law rather than continued American discrimination against members of historically oppressed groups.

If the goal of antidiscrimination law is not to remedy historically situated oppression, but merely to prevent or stop the utilization of race in laws or policies as a criterion for applicability, the ramifications for multiracial racialized persons seeking to bring cases of racial discrimination are clear. Those who racially identify as multiracial—having no legally established race—and therefore have no basis upon which to argue that any law discriminates against them. However, if the goal of antidiscrimination law is to remedy historically situated oppression, and evidence shows a history of antipathy directed at multiracial racialized persons *as* multiracial racialized persons, then multiracial racialized persons qualify as a suspect class and may use antidiscrimination law to protect themselves.

Toward a Distinctive Multiracial Group Identity

Scholarship in multiracial studies began establishing the features of a group identity for multiracial racialized Americans at least as early as the first half of the twentieth century. For example, during this period, Robert Park and Everett Verner Stonequist produced work on what they called the "marginal man," a person (typically mixed race, but who could also be a Jewish American or any sort of American immigrant) who, by virtue of being a member of at least two cultures, was perpetually outside of the mainstream (Park 1928, Stonequist 1937). Characteristic features of the marginal man were living in two worlds at once and living in a state of conflict. The marginal man was a "cultural hybrid," a person "living and sharing intimately in the cultural life and traditions of two distinct peoples, never quite willing to break, even if he were permitted to do so, with his past and his traditions, and not quite accepted in the new society in which he now sought to find a place. The marginal man was a person on the margin of two cultures and two societies, which never completely interpenetrated and fused" (Park 1928, 892).

What emerged was a distinctive personality type, a microcosm of cultural conflict, inherently ambiguous, and operating as a source of confusion and change for the surrounding, established cultures. Later theorists speculated on both the negative features of this personality type (e.g., a tendency to delinquency, maladjustment, insecurity, and emotional instability) and the positive features (e.g., high potential for originality and creativity, cosmopolitanism) (Goldberg 1941; Antonovsky 1956, Johnson 1960; Weisberger 1992; Grant and Breese 1997; Rockquemore and Brunsma 2002). Finally, the marginal man often brings a vantage point that is removed from both or all particularized vantage points, resulting in the honing of certain skills in mediation and translation.

In the mid-twentieth century, much scholarship was produced on the question of whether there were certain professional pursuits particularly suited for the "marginal man." Examples included the foreman (Gardiner and Whyte 1945; Wray 1949), the chiropractor (Wardwell 1952), the druggist (McCormack 1956), the merchant-marine radio operator (Record 1957), the university dean of student personnel (Nudd 1961), the engineering technician (Evan 1964), the integrative manager (Ziller, Stark, and Pruden 1969), the university labor educator (Nash 1978), and the academic general practitioner (Reid 1982). The consistent theme in these occupations was a person "either unable to attain acceptance in the roles to which they aspired" (Goldberg 2012, 207) or "trapped between two occupations or statuses in which they were considered outsiders" (ibid.).

Recent scholarship in multiracial studies has provided evidence of a long history of racially motivated antipathy against multiracial racialized persons in America that continues to the present day (Leong 2010; Campbell and Herman 2010).

A group identity can arguably be generated based on these shared experiences of multiracial antipathy. As noted above, the antipathy against multiracial racialized persons originated in the taboo against interracial relationships and interracial mixing between nonracialized persons and racialized persons. Incidents described in recent court cases provide proof that antipathy toward multiracial racialized persons continues to exist today. In one incident, described by the U.S. District Court for the Eastern District of Tennessee in passing, Oreo cookies were thrown onto a high school basketball court when a biracial student entered the game (*DeFoe v. Spiva,* 2010). In another federal court case, a nonracialized supervisor of a racialized employee who had multiracial racialized children is reported as having made a series of derisive remarks about the children directed at their status as multiracial racialized (*Green v. Franklin National Bank,* 2006). In yet another incident of multiracial animus described in a federal court case, not only were an employee's multiracial children subjected to multiracial slurs (e.g., "half-breed"), the employee herself was subjected to disparaging comments about her interracial relationship from her coworkers who at one point left a magazine article condemning interracial relationships in her desk drawer (*Wheaton v. North Oakland Medical Center*, 2005). In still another incident, an employee in an interracial marriage was subjected to "pervasive harassment"—a coworker remarking at one point that the employee had "ruined herself by marrying a black man and having biracial children" (*Madison v. IBP*, 2003)—including having her children referred to as "monkeys" and "zebras."

Many theorists of group rights argue that certain experiences of individual group members may be so related that a kind of solidarity is generated by these experiences that forms the basis of legally recognizable group rights (see, e.g., May 1987). This subjectivity-based argument in favor of group rights grants group rights to members when the people in the group understand themselves as bound together as members of a group (Galenkamp 1998; Segesvary 1995). The key is a strong sense of intragroup solidarity (ibid.). While the fact of understanding themselves as a group is subjective, in this view, the shared understanding is nonetheless based on objective factors such as a common history or social condition, or shared interests (May 1987). The shared history of antipathy toward multiracialism, or the shared intersubjective experience of having been discriminated against in virtue of their multiracial status, or the shared interest multiracial racialized persons have in protecting themselves from discrimination based on their multiracial status are all factors that can be understood as the kind of intersubjective experience that can form the basis for a legally recognizable racial group composed of those with multiracial ancestry.

AN ADDITIONAL MODIFICATION TO ANTIDISCRIMINATION LAW

There is a branch of late twentieth and early twenty-first century philosophy of race that has spent a significant amount of time debating whether race is "real." One strand of this branch of philosophy—often called the "eliminativist" position—has involved bringing into the philosophical mainstream evidence (available since at least the 1950s) to the effect that race as it is commonly understood to exist (i.e., as having a basis in biology) is not supported by scientific evidence (Zack 1993, 2002, 2010; Appiah 1993; Piper 1992; Piper 1992–1993). For the eliminativists, belief in the existence of biological race is thought to be the core misconception driving racial oppression. This is because, for the eliminativist, a belief in biological race carries with it at least two related beliefs: (1) the belief that there is a correlation between somatic traits (like hair texture, eye shape, or skin color) and character or personality traits (like intelligence or trustworthiness), and (2) the belief in a kind of natural racial hierarchy according to which some races are superior to other races. The assumption behind the eliminativist position is that once racial hierarchy is exposed as lacking in scientific support, those holding racist views and engaging in racially oppressive practices will suddenly stop the offending practices. The eliminativists maintain, then, that in order to end racial oppression, we should eliminate "race talk" or "race thinking" because continuing to speak of race or think about race at all perpetuates the misconception that race has a biological basis, to the detriment of efforts to curb racism. Many advocates for the rights of multiracial racialized persons advocate the eliminativist position. In their view, any talk at all of race invokes the biological conception of race, and invocation of the biological concept of race undermines the interests of multiracial racialized persons.

There are ways of thinking about race other than in terms of biology, however. Another strand of contemporary philosophy of race emphasizes the social—as opposed to the biological—existence of race, building upon the evidence that biological race is unsupported by scientific evidence but acknowledging nonetheless that race operates very powerfully in our lives. From this "social constructionism" viewpoint, concepts of race "are the products of the socio-historical practices, behaviors, conventions, and institutions that give rise to them" (Atkin 2012, 47), providing race with an ontological status that is significant, if not fixed or unchangeable (Taylor 2004; Shelby 2005).

An interesting twist on social constructionism—sometimes called "reconstructionism"—incorporates what is known as "racial realism" or a concession to the permanence of racism (Bell 1992b) as a key aspect of the philosophical examination of the phenomenon of race. For the racial realist, it is of no moment whether race exists biologically, socially, or any other way since regardless of the outcome of that inquiry, racism is alive and well. The racial realist disentangles the problem of racial oppression from the question of whether or not race is "real" to focus instead on improving conditions for racialized minority groups (Bell 1992b). The racial reconstructionist adds to the (weak) social constructionist position a recommendation that the concept of race should be used to actually improve conditions for members of racialized minority groups rather than used in the service of oppressing them.

As long as there is a need for racial antidiscrimination law, there is a need for utilization of the concept of race. As this chapter points out, there is much evidence to show that such a need exists today. Such utilization will not lead, as eliminitavists and some multiracial racialized persons fear, to the reification of the concept of pure, biological races so long as the sociohistorical concept of race is identified as the concept of race that should be at work in antidiscrimination law. In this sociohistorical concept of race, the reality of race is not rooted in biology but in historically situated social practices, behaviors, conventions, and institutions. In other words, what makes race real is the fact that a given society or culture acts and behaves as if it is real, resulting in very tangible consequences in the lives of those who have been racialized.

Within the realm of antidiscrimination law, then, in order to identify a group that should be granted the status of a "suspect class" (or a group deserving of special protection under antidiscrimination laws), the relevant test is not what biology might tell us, but history. Has the group in question been the subject of widespread, institutionalized, systematized, and legalized oppression or subjugation based on the identifying group characteristic or not? If so, such a group qualifies as a "suspect class." This would include multiracial racialized Americans, given the history outlined above. Note that within this framework, whether race is biologically real or not is completely irrelevant. The question is whether race has been treated as if it were real historically, and if so, whether that treatment has resulted in the oppression of the members of the group in question, in this case multiracial racialized persons.

CONCLUDING REFLECTIONS

Multiracial racialized persons currently have no protection under U.S. laws from racial discrimination directed at them by virtue of their multiracial status, despite a long history of such discrimination in the U.S. legal system and in American society at large. The surface reason for this lack of protection is that antidiscrimination law requires a prospective plaintiff to first identify as a member of one and only one of five legally established racial groups: Asian, "black," Latino/a, Native American, or "white." In the eyes of U.S. courts, in other words, multiracial racialized persons do not constitute what the law calls a "suspect class" (i.e., a group having a history of discrimination), nor can a law that discriminates against multiracial racialized persons constitute what the law calls a "suspect classification" (or a constitutionally impermissible basis for distinguishing one person from another, vis-à-vis access to employment opportunities or other social goods of various sorts). The deeper reason, however, is that U.S. Courts no longer acknowledge that the purpose of antidiscrimination law—with regard to cases of racial discrimination—is to provide redress for historically situated, systematized racial oppression. If American courts were to acknowledge this, then a good case could be made for multiracial racialized persons' being legally established as what the law calls a "suspect class" for the same reasons that monoracial minority groups have been acknowledged as "suspect classes." However, since the courts have moved from discussing antidiscrimination cases in terms of "suspect classes" to discussing them in terms of "suspect classifications," an alternative option to protect multiracial racialized persons from racial discrimination would be for the courts to acknowledge multiracialism as a legally established racial identity.

The argument for the recognition of multiracial racialized persons as a "suspect class" is rooted in a shared history of systemic and legalized oppression directed at multiracial racialized persons in virtue of their multiraciality Examples of this oppression include the long history of antimiscegenation laws in the United States (which go as far back as the seventeenth century), widespread enactment of Jim Crow (segregation) laws enacted after *Plessy v. Ferguson,* and the rise of the "one-drop" rule and the phenomenon of hypodescent in American society and in U.S. laws, according to which people with any known minority group ancestry were categorized as members of the minority racial group in question. The oppression continues to this day through the persistence in American society and American courts of a belief in biological race, together with its concomitant features of racial purity and racial essentialism. This belief maintains that human races exist, are pure, are biologically based, and are associated with specific physical and nonphysical traits that cannot be escaped. Within this framework, not only do multiracial racialized persons not have rights, *they don't exist* as a first order of business. More importantly, for their ability to avail themselves of antidiscrimination law, multiracial racialized persons *have no legally established racial identity*.

Scholarship in multiracial studies, however, suggests that multiracial racialized persons do indeed have a group identity rooted in their multiracialism. This identity is forged in the crucible of belonging to at least two cultures or races at once, of feeling pulled between these two cultures or races, of being a "cultural hybrid," and of never quite being accepted in either or any specific race or culture. The multiracial racialized person's identity is marginal, peripheral, a microcosm of cultural conflict, inherently ambiguous and operating as a source of confusion and change for the surrounding, established cultures.

Most importantly for antidiscrimination law, however, the long history of shared experiences of having been oppressed or discriminated against in virtue of their multiracial status (a set of experiences that continues today) provides the basis upon which multiracial racialized persons might successfully argue that they have rights as a group and therefore qualify as a "suspect class." These experiences include name-calling ("half-breed"), disparaging remarks about oneself or one's children, and a lack of support from one or all monoracial groups to which one might belong. Systematic alienation from the body of laws designed to protect all people from racial discrimination (in virtue of a failure on the part of the law to legally recognize multiracial identity), however, may be the greatest basis upon which to argue in favor of legal protection for multiracial racialized persons as multiracial racialized persons. At a minimum, then, U.S. antidiscrimination law must begin to acknowledge multiracial identity as a legally established racial status. In order to do so, however, it must first acknowledge that race is sociocultural and sociohistorical rather than biological (categorical). As antidiscrimination law currently, operates, without this step, U.S. law is in the awkward position of allowing nonracialized persons to bring cases of racial discrimination but not multiracial racialized persons.

In chapter 5, I have tried to highlight the problems with using biological race in equal protection law through demonstrating the nonsensical results of using this concept of race to address racial discrimination against multiracial racialized persons. I have made the case for the problems with biological race as applied to multiracial racialized persons through juxtaposing the very real racial discrimination multiracial racialized persons experience with the fact that their racial identity does not fold well into the arbitrary racial categories that antidiscrimination law currently presumes are both real and definitive. The impression I hope to have left is that the way race in general is processed in antidiscrimination law is out of touch with the reality of how race works on the ground, that is, in the world. Racial identity in the United States (as is the case everywhere) is socially constructed, arbitrary, capricious, and nonsensical, having absolutely no basis in anything other than the judgment calls of the makers of meaning and laws, i.e., those in power. To the extent that racial identity does have meaning or reality, it is through the group identity and cohesion that is generated through shared experiences, shared values, and shared goals. Racial discrimination and oppression is therefore the imposition of the badge of inferiority and powerlessness on persons whom those in power wish to remain disempowered. From this point of view, racial discrimination per se, color-blindness, and "reverse racism" are absurd, nonsensical and ridiculous phenomena, not aiming at equality but tilting at windmills.

NOTES

1. This chapter is based on a book chapter titled, "Multiracial Americans and Racial Discrimination," originally published in *Race Policy and Multiracial Americans*, Kathleen Korgen, Ed. Bristol, UK: Policy Press. January 2016, pp. 81–100, reprinted here by permission of Policy Press.

2. I refer to such persons as "multiracial racialized" persons to highlight both (1) the fact that such persons have nonracialized as well as racialized ancestry which they include into their racial self-concept, and (2) that such persons are simultaneously simply a branch of racialized persons more broadly, owing to the one-drop rule and its legacy (more on the one-drop rule later in this chapter). Arguably, of course, a large majority of racialized persons in the United States (if not all) have nonracialized ancestors, owing to the history of forced racial "mixing" between masters and slaves during the slavery era. It is only those persons who are aware of and identify with their nonracialized ancestry who would fall into the category "multiracial racialized" for purposes of this chapter.

3. Mention of "racial groups," "races," "blacks," "whites," "the black race," or "the white race" and similar terms in this chapter should not be construed as an endorsement of the popularly held belief in American society in the existence of biologically based, pure, human races characterized by biological essentialism. Instead, the bare terms have been used as a convenient shorthand for "so-called racial groups," "so-called races," "so-called blacks," "so-called whites," the "so-called black race," the "so-called white race," etc.

SIX

Thoughts Moving Forward

To a certain extent, this book can be construed as an effort in the project to bring juridicopolitical theory out of the clouds and onto the ground where the people live, out of Plato's intelligible realm and into the hearts, minds, and bodies of those of us here on Earth. After all, as many of the theorists I have utilized in the book have suggested, what good are rights if they are not respected (Darby 2009)? What good is the law if it operates against the interests of those least advantaged, particularly through the unconscious prejudices of elites (Lawrence 1995)? What good is justice if it is "just" for "us" (the nonracialized, the powerful, the elites) (Mills 1997; Bell 1980)? As may be evident from the content of the book so far, although I have articulated the topic of this book as the meaning of the Equal Protection Clause, what the book is really about is why, over 150 years after the end of slavery and over 60 years after the decision in *Brown v. Board of Education*, racialized persons still live in a state of extreme inequality as compared to their nonracialized contemporaries. A brief discussion of what is known as the Three-fifths Compromise might shed light on this question.

Despite having fought in the Continental Army, racialized persons were considered three-fifths of a person under the Three-fifths Compromise enacted in 1787, for purposes of determining State representation in the U.S. House of Representatives (Finkelman 2001). Interestingly, however, it was the *Northern* states who wanted slaves to count for 0 percent of a person each, arguing that slaves were property, and the *Southern* states who wanted slaves to count for 100 percent of a person each. The reason the nonslaveholders (by and large) wanted slaves not to count as persons at all and the slaveholders (by and large) wanted slaves to count as full persons was because the more persons one had in one's state, the more power the state had in the federal government. The "Compromise," then of counting slaves as a little more than half a person each (resulting in the Southern states having more say in the federal government than they otherwise might have) was a victory for the slaveholders over the racialized persons they enslaved. This is because although the bodies of racialized persons counted toward giving the states in which they resided power, racialized persons themselves had *no power,* since they themselves were unable to vote. The story of the Three-fifths Compromise is being mentioned here at the close of this book on racial equality because it typifies the kind of liberal legal jurisprudence that results in equality violations of the oppressed. The Three-fifths Compromise is typical of liberal legal jurisprudence because of its nonsensical origins, the banality of its creation (a mere compromise between two different extreme views), as well as the devastating symbolic and tangible effect it had on the social status of racialized persons in the United States. The Three-Fifths Compromise is arguably a shining symbol of liberal legal theory at work, the jewel in the crown of the white supremacy that is the business-as-usual of United States politics, the poster child of "legal equality" with its obvious origins in Aristotelian proportional equality and clear presumption of the biological otherness and inferiority of those legally deemed less than fully human.

It was not until the Thirteenth Amendment (abolishing slavery) was enacted that the Three-fifths compromise was rendered obsolete (Finkelman 2001). As mentioned earlier in this book, the Thirteenth Amendment was one of three "Civil War Amendments" (a.k.a. the Reconstruction Amendments), all enacted just after the end of the American Civil War. The other two amendments, as mentioned earlier in chapter 2, were the Fifteenth Amendment, which prohibited discrimination in voting "on account of race, color, or previous condition of servitude," and the Fourteenth Amendment, which addressed the rights of citizenship and equal protection of the laws, proposed in response to issues former slaves were experiencing after the war. One could say that the Civil War Amendments, in a sense, repealed the Three-fifths Compromise. They stood for the proposition that *in the face of the radical break with morality that was the institution of chattel slavery,* a corrective was in order to such a high degree that three Constitutional amendments were in order. Ideal theory did not work, so it was time to try something else. That something else was an engagement with the problem of social/racial inequality through a change in federal law.

So, this book can be construed as a sort of critique of ideal theory through the usage of a sample case: the Equal Protection Clause. Its subthesis is that the Equal Protection Clause has been distorted and disfigured at the hands of the highly idealized liberal legal theory. Ideal theory, of course, is the approach to juridicopolitical philosophy, first articulated (but arguably not originated) by John Rawls, that stresses the need to work with idealizations in order to come up with a conception of a fully just (or equal) society (Rawls 1971; Rawls 1996). John Rawls explicitly defined his work as ideal theory, stating that idealizations uniquely enabled the crafter of a theory of justice to gain a "systemic grasp" on the relevant issues (Rawls 1971, 8). In ideal theory, we begin by asking "what a perfectly just society would be like" and once that is established, only then can we get to the business of addressing specific problems in existing societies that undermine the achievement of such a society.

But, for critics of ideal theory like Charles Mills, the idea that we can create a just society from an idealized model is naïve, even dangerous. Mills explains, "Factually, idealization involves attribution to the agents (as conceived of in the theory) human capacities significantly deviant from the norm: for example, their degrees of rationality, self-knowledge, ability to make interpersonal cardinal utility comparisons, and the like" (Mills 2005, 167–68). Mills continues, "What distinguishes ideal theory" from non-ideal theories, however, "is the reliance on idealization to the exclusion, or at least marginalization, of the actual" (168). We indulge ourselves in ideal theory, in other words, at the expense of dealing with reality. In the service of clarity, Mills then lays out the basic concepts and assumptions of ideal theory: (1) an idealized social ontology that "assume[s] the abstract and undifferentiated equal atomic individuals of classical liberalism" (168), (2) idealized capabilities in which human agents "have completely unrealistic capacities attributed to them" (ibid.) (e.g., the ability to be morally perfect), (3) silence on oppression, including on the way "systematic oppression is likely to shape the basic social institutions" (168–69), (4) ideal social institutions, "with little or no sense of how their actual workings may systematically disadvantage women, the poor, and [racialized persons]" (169), and (5) an idealized cognitive sphere in which "the consequences of oppression . . . will typically not be recognized, let alone theorized" (ibid.), and strict compliance, where "[e]veryone is presumed to act justly and to do [their] part in upholding just institutions" (ibid.) á la Rawls.

In the case of the present interpretation of the Equal Protection Clause, which relies heavily on the false concept of biological race and the insidiously oppressive concept of legal equality, the *ideal* that racial justice can be achieved by the unreflective outlawing of racial classifications per se (except in extreme circumstances) arguably meets all of Mill's criteria. The idealized social ontology is that persons of all races are socially equal, and treated with the equal dignity and respect that would justify relinquishment of the remedial purpose of the Equal Protection Clause. The idealized capabilities are the beliefs that none of those charging "reverse racism" are motivated by antiblack racism themselves. As mentioned extensively in this book, the current interpretation of the Equal Protection Clause is completely silent on the history of oppression that necessitated the enactment of the Fourteenth Amendment in the first place. Finally, it is certainly the case that the current interpretation of the

Clause presumes that all involved in the problem of continuing racial inequality are doing their part to uphold the institutions that theoretically support and maintain the fictitious racial equality ideal theory presumes exists here in the so-called post-racial era.

But here in the real world, none of the relevant idealizations are actualized, and the result is profound disconnect between the law and reality. Instead of a clear, cohesive body of equal protection law that reliably guides Supreme Court Justices (and others) in the development of good law, we have instead a series of interpretations of the Equal Protection Clause over the years that are inconsistent with each other, and that leave us today without a way to provide redress for the kind of racial discrimination the Equal Protection Clause was designed to address.

I identify and formulate four major interpretations of the Equal Protection Clause over the years. These interpretations are as follows: (1) that the Equal Protection Clause protects racialized persons only, prevalent from about 1873 to 1895, (2) that "equal" in the Equal Protection Clause means separate, from about 1896 to 1953, (3) that there are groups of people who deserve special protection from discriminatory laws, popular from about 1954 to about 1973, and (4) that the Equal Protection Clause protects all from racial discrimination per se, prevalent from about 1978 to the present. These interpretations, and the cases corresponding to them, are listed in table 6.1.

According to my schematization, Interpretation #1 is the interpretation that most closely maps the intentions of the drafters of the Clause, and Interpretation #4 is the interpretation that has been utilized by the Supreme Court since the late 1970s. Each interpretation between the two extremes represents a reaction to the one previous to it. For example, Interpretation #2, Separate But Equal Doctrine (discussed in chapter 2), entails a form of full blown legal equality. With *Plessy v. Ferguson* (1896), we have the Supreme Court openly stating that racial segregation is consistent with the Equal Protection Clause. Interpretation #3, however, Certain Groups Protected, briefly reverts to the original interpretation in striking down numerous laws that adversely affect racialized persons, soon followed by Interpretation #4, the penultimate legal equality formulation, which invents "reverse discrimination," finds it unconstitutional, and simultaneously starts a string of decisions that protect the nonracialized more than the racialized.

My formulation of the different eras is fairly standard, although others draw the lines separating the different interpretive eras slightly differently, depending upon their scholarly project.

For example, legal historian Michael Klarman divides up the various interpretations according to historical era and makes the (Critical Legal Studies?) case that constitutional decisions are more a function of the "social and political times" than anything definitive or binding about what the law does or should mean (Klarman 2004, 5). Klarman writes,

Table 6.1. Major Supreme Court Interpretations of the Equal Protection Clause

Era	*Cases*	*Interpretation*
Interpretation #1 Clause Protects Racialized Persons Only (1868–1895)	*The Slaughterhouse Cases* (1873), *Strauder v. West Virginia* (1880), *The Civil Rights Cases* (1875).	Clause applies to ex-slaves (racialized persons) only.
Interpretation #2 Separate But Equal (1896–1953)	*Plessy v. Ferguson* (1896), *Missouri ex rel. Gaines v. Canada* (1938), *Korematsu v. U.S.* (1944), *McLaurin v. OK State Regents* (1950), *Sweatt v. Painter* (1950).	"Equal" in equal protection can mean separate; Separate usually means inferior.
Interpretation #3 Certain Groups Protected (1954–1973)	*Brown v. Board of Education* (1954), *Brown II* (1955), *Loving v. Virginia* (1967), *Alexander v. Holmes Co. Brd. of Ed.* (1969), *Swann v. Charlotte-Mecklenburg Brd. of Ed.* (1971).	Separate But Equal overturned; "all deliberate speed" changes to desegregation "at once"; anti-miscegenation laws violate the EPC; busing approved to overcome segregation: strict scrutiny appropriate level of review in race cases.
Interpretation #4 Racial Discrimination Per Se Is the Problem (1976–present)	*Washington v. Davis* (1976), *Regents of the University of California v. Bakke* (1978), *Fullilove v. Klutznick* (1980), *City of Richmond v. J.A. Croson Company* (1989), *Adarand Constructors, Inc. v. Peña* (1995), *Gratz v. Bollinger* (2003), *Grutter v. Bollinger* (2003).	Discriminatory impact not enough to invalidate law. Laws containing racial "classifications" are discriminatory; Dissent in *Fullilove* stresses that all racial classifications unconstitutional; *Croson* holds that a minority set-aside program excluding nonracialized persons violates the EPC; *Adarand* holds that all racial classifications are unconstitutional; *Michigan Cases* together hold that race-conscious programs must be "narrowly tailored."

"This book argues that because constitutional law is generally quite indeterminate, constitutional interpretation almost inevitably reflects the broader social and political context of the times" (ibid.) than anything more substantive. Klarman begins his analysis with the *Plessy* era. For Klarman, in the *Plessy* era (i.e., the era of *Plessy v. Ferguson*, roughly 1895–1910) laws that segregated persons on the basis of race were perfectly constitutional as long as the races were treated "equally." To help flesh out how the social context influenced the Court's decision in *Plessy*, Klarman discusses how racial segregation, at the time, was believed to be a *valid exercise of the state's power to promote health, safety and morals* (Klarman 2004, 21). For example, in 1883, the Court rejected an equal protection challenge to a statute that punished fornication more severely when the parties were of different races than when they were of the same race. The Court emphasized that the law treated both parties to interracial fornication the same (*Pace v. Alabama* [1883]). This interpretation of the Clause (Separate But Equal Doctrine) was supported by the views of "large blocs of whites" who at the time opposed the social equality of racialized persons (ibid.).

In the Progressive Era, roughly the 1910s, according to Klarman, the Court struck down many laws that discriminated against racialized persons. These included peonage laws that coerced primarily the labor of racialized persons, a law that excluded racialized persons from luxury accommodations, a law that effectively exempted illiterate nonracialized persons from voting literacy tests through a grandfather clause that exempted those persons and their descendants who were enfranchised before 1867, and a law that segregated neighborhood blocks by race. Klarman speculates that one explanation for this state of affairs is that "even in the depths of Progressive Era racism, national opinion still supported formal compliance with constitutional norms, which is all that these rulings really required" (Klarman 2004, 62). Importantly for Klarman, Progressive Era race decisions proved inconsequential. Since the laws were concerned more with form than substance, they were easy to circumvent. For example, the invalidation of the grandfather clause enfranchised no racialized persons.

Between the First and Second World Wars ("The InterWar Period"), or between 1920 and 1937, the Court decided cases that made new law protecting the rights of racialized persons, but only to intervene against the worst abuses of Jim Crow, such as laws allowing the execution of innocent racialized persons based on forcibly extracted confessions in corrupt courtrooms, resolving schemes that barred racialized persons from participating in Democratic primaries, invalidated residential segregation ordinances, and invalidated a state law that provided racialized persons who wished to pursue graduate or professional education with scholarships to attend universities outside of the state. The Court was not in the habit, during this period, of challenging "the more routine but fundamental aspects of white supremacy, such as segregation and disenfranchisement," however (Klarman 2004, 99).

The World War II era, roughly the 1940s, contained much progress, according to Klarman. During this time period, with regard to voting, the Court invalidated Oklahoma's effort to grandfather its grandfather clause related to voting, struck down Texas's "white" primary, and condemned the exclusion of racialized persons from pre-primary elections conducted by a "private" political club in east Texas. With regard to education, the Court required Oklahoma to provide qualified racialized persons with in-state legal education, ordered that a racialized man should be admitted to the University of Texas School of Law because a recently created black law school was not equal, and forbade the education school of the University of Oklahoma from segregating a black student in dining, library, and classroom facilities. With regard to housing, the Court ruled that injunctions enforcing racially restrictive covenants were unconstitutional. In transportation, the Court twice interpreted the Interstate Commerce Act to bar railroads from denying racialized persons equal luxury accommodations, and also invalidated a bus segregation law's application to interstate passengers. With regard to criminal procedure, the Court upheld earlier rulings requiring the state to appoint counsel for indigent defendants, that barred race discrimination in jury selection, and that overturned convictions based on coerced confessions (Klarman 2004, 172–73).

In the School Desegregation era, roughly the 1950s, according to Klarman, the social and political context on the topic of racial segregation had changed dramatically since the early twentieth century when "radical racist" James Vardaman had openly proclaimed, in his campaign to become governor of South Carolina that "every Negro in the state will be lynched," if necessary, to maintain white supremacy (Klarman 2004, 64). Several million racialized persons had migrated from the south to northern cities in search of economic opportunities and racial tolerance (Klarman 2004, 290). Demographic shifts had produced a racialized, urban middle class with education, disposable income, and an inclination to social protest. The war against fascism encouraged many Americans to reconsider their racial views, in particular to clarify differences between Nazi Germany and the Jim Crow south (Klarman 2004, 291). Then, in 1954—that is, within this social context—the Supreme Court decided *Brown v. Board of Education*, according to which racial segregation in public schools was unanimously invalidated on equal protection grounds.

Klarman discusses the era of *Brown* in the context of the civil rights movement, including social forces at work both before and after the decision in *Brown*, in such a way as to highlight that, although, arguably, *Brown v. Board of Education* was the most important Court decision of the twentieth century in that it officially overturned the Separate But Equal Doctrine, *at the same time the decision in Brown had very little practical effect.* Even before *Brown*, some northern states that had many formally segregated school districts began to desegregate; four western states—Arizona, New Mexico, Kansas, and Wyoming—had also begun eradicating segregation before *Brown*, with the Court's legal intervention merely accelerating the process. "Border states," such as Delaware, Maryland, West Virginia, and Missouri, likely would have desegregated even without legal intervention. Klarman writes, "*Brown* pushed against an open door in these states" (Klarman 2004, 345).

The eleven states of the former Confederacy responded to *Brown* very differently. Most notably, virtually no desegregation at all occurred until 1957. Although the pace of *de jure* (legal) desegregation increased in the early 1960s as lawsuits proliferated and federal judges grew less tolerant of delay, *by 1963 only 1.06 percent of southern racialized students attended desegregated schools* (Klarman 2004, 349), and nowhere in the south had desegregation moved very far into rural areas (ibid.). There was a backlash, in other words, against desegregation of public schools in the deep south. Southern politics became radicalized, with leading candidates for office taking extreme segregationist positions, "turning 'moderation' into a derisive term" (Klarman 2004, 351). For a brief stint, the pace of (*de jure*) school desegregation accelerated during the civil rights movement. Nonetheless, "when Congress passed the 1964 Civil Rights Act, only one black child in a hundred in the South attended a racially mixed school" (Klarman 2004, 362). Soon thereafter, the percentage of southern racialized children in desegregated schools shot up to 16.9 percent in 1967 and roughly 90 percent in 1973, leading many to conclude that it was the civil rights movement, not *Brown*, that caused the most school desegregation in the south (Klarman 2004, 363).[1]

So, here at the end of our journey into the meaning of the Equal Protection Clause, and in light of the changes I have recommended to Supreme Court thinking on the topics of race and equality so as to render the Clause more useful in the service of racial justice in the United States, it seems incumbent upon me to take notice of the fact that it very well may be that the recommended changes in the way the Court thinks about race and equality will not be well received by the Supreme Court, here in the age of Trump. As I write these final words, there are white supremacist marches and "free speech" rallies taking place all over the country, in a number and to a degree of open disregard for racial harmony that this country has not seen since before the civil rights movement.

Maybe there is no hope for America. Maybe Obama was wrong. Maybe Americans are destined to be mired in the ugliness and ignorance of racial hatred forever. The idea that racism is a permanent feature of American society that cannot be eliminated (through law or any other means) is certainly a foundational concept in Critical Race Theory. According to the late Derrick Bell, it is a waste of time to attempt to eliminate American racism since it is a part of what he calls the "racial consciousness" of America (Bell 1992b). Instead, racialized persons should focus on, as Howard McGary has recommended, the social problems that racialized persons face as a group and on the specifics of how to solve those problems themselves (McGary 1999). Instead of fighting a losing battle against racism, perhaps the resources of racialized persons should be galvanized and strengthened so they can meet their own needs, with the added bonus of the self-esteem that comes from doing so. For Bell and McGary, self-determination is the path out of social inequality and toward social equality for racialized persons.

But, even Derrick Bell thinks a change in the laws can operate to support the social equality of racialized persons if what he calls "interest convergence" is present. For Bell, "interest convergence" is the idea that if a law or policy operates for the benefit of both racialized persons *and nonracialized persons*, the law has a chance of succeeding with the nonracialized majority. If such interest convergence can be made manifest, then progress toward racial equality can be made. Recall from above that Bell explains that although in *Brown v. Board of Education*, as was the case with the abolition of slavery, there were nonracialized persons for whom recognition of racial equality was sufficient motivation, as was the case with abolition, "the number [of nonracialized persons] who would act on *morality alone* was insufficient to bring about the desired racial reform" (Bell 1999, 23). It was *other* nonracialized persons who gave desegregation its legs and its power. In addition to racialized persons and nonracialized persons who accepted the moral imperative of racial equality, there were also *nonracialized* persons who had (primarily economic) interests in desegregation. There were also *nonracialized* persons who saw the potential of transforming the south from a "rural plantation" to the Sunbelt with huge potential for profits, but only if the south dropped its distracting struggle to maintain racial segregation. In other words, the reason *Brown* was decided in favor of racial equality was that *Brown* supported the economic interests of a large number of nonracialized persons. There was "interest convergence" between nonracialized capitalists and racialized persons in the quest for the desegregation of public schools.

If Bell is right, then changing the way the Supreme Court interprets the Equal Protection Clause so as to accept that race is sociocultural (and not biological) and that social equality (and not legal equality) is the proper goal of equal protection law will not occur unless a significant benefit to nonracialized persons can be identified as a likely result of changing the law in this way. On the question of how nonracialized persons might benefit from an equal protection law that actually operates to address racial equality, Carina Fourie is on to something, I think, when she points out that social inequality hurts higher-status persons as much as lower-status persons, in the form of a loss of affiliation, and a diminished quality of life. Along this train of thought, perhaps large numbers of nonracialized persons will be motivated by an improved quality of life sufficiently to support the rejection of "reverse discrimination" as a legitimate constitutional argument. However, while I would like to believe "affiliation" would be sufficient motivation for nonracialized persons to reject "reverse discrimination," I am a realist enough to know that this will surely never occur. However, there may be other ways that "reverse discrimination" hurts nonracialized persons. The optimist in me thinks these ways can be found.

Here, at the end of this book, then, it seems to me, against Derrick Bell, that the goal of racial equality is within our sights. I do not think the evidence shows that racism is permanent. By any measure, the phenomenon has surely lessened (however slightly) as time has passed since the end of slavery. However, as with any attempt to convince someone to do anything that is not, at first blush, in their interests to do, the challenge will be to find a legitimate (preferably economic, if Bell is right) basis for nonracialized persons to conclude that eliminating "reverse discrimination" is in their interests. I will likely write a follow-up to this book that will set out to meet that challenge. Stay tuned for my thoughts on this important question in my never-ending battle for racial equality in the United States.

NOTE

1. Of specific importance, for Klarman, was the 1964 Civil Rights Act, a key piece of legislation in the movement.

Bibliography

BOOKS AND ARTICLES

Alcoff, Linda M. 2006. *Visible Identities: Race, Gender, and the Self.* Oxford: Oxford University Press.

Anderson, Elizabeth S. 1999. "What Is the Point of Equality?" *Ethics: An International Journal of Social, Political, and Legal Philosophy* 109(2): 287–337.

———. 2010. *The Imperative of Integration*, Princeton: Princeton University Press.

Antonovsky, Aaron. 1956. "Toward a Refinement of the 'Marginal Man' Concept." *Social Forces* 35(1): 57–62.

Appiah, K. A. 1992. *In My Father's House. Africa in the Philosophy of Culture*. New York: Oxford University Press.

Arendt, Hannah. 1963. *Eichmann in Jerusalem: A Report on the Banality of Evil*. New York: Viking Press.

Aristotle, Terence H. Irwin and Gail Fine. 1995. *Aristotle: Selections*. Indianapolis: Hackett Publishing.

Aristotle, and F. H. Peters. 1997. *The Nicomachean Ethics of Aristotle*. New York, NY: Classics of Liberty Library.

Aristotle, and R. Crisp. 2014. *Nicomachean Ethics*. Cambridge & New York: Cambridge University Press.

Atkin, Albert. 2012. *The Philosophy of Race*. Durham & Bristol: Acumen Publishing.

Baer, Judith A. 1983. *Equality under the Constitution: Reclaiming the Fourteenth Amendment*. Ithaca: Cornell University Press.

Balkin, Jack M., and Reva B. Siegel. 2003–2004. "The American Civil Rights Tradition: Anticlassification or Antisubordination?" 58 *U. Miami L. Rev.* 9.

Banton, Michael. 1988. *Racial Consciousness*. London, New York: Longman.

Bell, Derrick. 1973. *Race, Racism, and American Law*. Boston, Toronto: Little, Brown and Company.

———. 1976. "Serving Two Masters: Integration Ideals and Client Interests in School Desegregation Litigation," 85 *Yale L.J.* 470.

———. 1980. "*Brown v. Board of Education* and the Interest-Convergence Dilemma" 93 *Harv. L. Rev.* 518.

———. 1992a. *Faces at the Bottom of the Well: The Permanence of Racism*. New York: Basic Books.

———. 1992b. "Racial Realism." 24 *Conn. L. Rev.* 363.

———. 1999. "*Brown v. Board of Education* and the Interest Convergence Dilemma." In *Critical Race Theory: The Key Writings That Formed the Movement*, Kimberlé Crenshaw, Neil Gotanda, Gary Peller, and Kendall Thomas, editors, 20–29. New York: The New Press (first published at 93 *Harv. Law Rev.* 518 [1980]).

———. 2004. "The Interest-Convergence Covenants." In *Silent Covenants*. Oxford & New York: Oxford University Press.

Bernasconi, Robert. 1992. "Locke's Almost Random Talk of Man: The Double Use of Words in the Natural Law Justification of Slavery." *Perspektiven Der Philosophie* 18: 293–318.

Bernasconi, Robert, and Tommie L. Lott, eds. 2000. *The Idea of Race*. Indianapolis/Cambridge: Hackett Publishing Company, Inc.

Bickel, Alexander M. 1955. "The Original Understanding and the Segregation Decision." 69 *Harvard Law Review* 1.

Binder, Guyora, and Robert Weisberg. 2000. *Literary Criticisms of Law*. Princeton, NJ: Princeton University Press.

Blumenbach, Johann F. 2000. "Of the Natural Variety of Mankind." In *The Idea of Race*, Robert Bernasconi and Tommy L. Lott, eds., 27–37. Indianapolis/Cambridge: Hackett Publishing Company, Inc.

Bobbit, Phillip. 1996, 1999. "Constitutional Law and Interpretation." In *A Companion to Philosophy of Law and Legal Theory*, ed. Dennis Patterson. Malden, MA: Blackwell Publishing.

Bonilla-Silva, Eduardo. 2010. *Racism Without Racists: Color-Blind Racism and Racial Inequality in Contemporary America*. Lanham, MD: Rowman & Littlefield.

(Botts) Tina Fernandes. 2013. "Antidiscrimination Law and the Multiracial Experience: A Reply to Nancy Leong." 10 *Hastings Race and Poverty Law Journal*. 191.

———. 2014. "Legal Hermeneutics." *Internet Encyclopedia of Philosophy*. ISSN 2161-0002. http://www.iep.utm.edu/leg-herm/, March 2018.

Brenner, Joel, and Liz Spayd. 1993. "Separate and Unequal: Racial Discrimination in Area Home Lending." *Washington Post*. 6–8 June: A1.

Brunsma, David L., and Kerry Ann Rockquemore. 2002. "What Does 'Black' Mean? Exploring the Epistemological Stranglehold of Racial Categorization." 28 *Critical Soc*. 101.

Campbell, Mary E., and Melissa Herman. 2010. "Politics and Policies: Attitudes Toward Multiracial Americans." *Ethnic and Racial Studies* 33(9): 1511–36.

Campos, Paul. 1992. "Against Constitutional Theory." *Yale Journal of Law and the Humanities* Vol. 4: Iss. 2, Article 4.

Chafe, William Henry et al., eds. 2001. *Remembering Jim Crow: African Americans Tell about Life in the Segregated South*. New York: New Press.

Christman, John. 2002. *Social and Political Philosophy: A Contemporary Introduction*, London and New York: Routledge.

Collins, Chuck, Amy Gluckman, Betsy Leondar-Wright, Meizhu Lui, Amy Offner, and Adria Scharf, eds. 2004. *The Wealth Inequality Reader*. Cambridge, MA: The Economic Affairs Bureau.

Cong. Globe, 39th Cong., 1st Sess. 2459. 1866.

Crenshaw, Kimberlé, Neil Gotanda, Gary Peller, and Kendall Thomas, editors. 2010. *Critical Race Theory: The Key Writings That Formed the Movement*. New York: The New Press.

Cudd, Ann E. 2006. *Analyzing Oppression*. New York: Oxford University Press.

Daniel, G. Reginald. 2002. *More Than Black? Multiracial Identity and the New Racial Order*. Philadelphia: Temple University Press.

———. 2007. *Race and Multiraciality in Brazil and the United States: Converging Paths?* University Park: Pennsylvania State University Press.

Darby, Derrick. 2009. *Rights, Race, and Recognition*. Cambridge: Cambridge University Press.

Darwin, Charles. 1871/2008. *On the Origin of Species*. New York: Sterling.

Darwin, Charles, and Mark Ridley. 1996. *The Darwin Reader*. New York: Norton.

Davies, John D. 1955. *Phrenology: Fad and Science, Nineteenth-Century American Crusade*. Hamden, CT: Archon.

Davis, F. James. 1991. *Who Is Black? One Nation's Definition*. University Park: The Pennsylvania State University Press.

Dedman, Bill. 1988. "The Color of Money: Mortgage Lending Practices Discriminate Against Blacks." *Atlanta Journal and Constitution* (May): 15–19.

Du Bois, W. E. B. 1897/2001. "The Conservation of Races." In *The American Negro Academy, Occasional Papers, no. 2*. Washington, DC, reprinted in *Race*, Robert Bernasconi, ed., 84–91. Malden and Oxford: Blackwell Publishers.

Du Bois, W. E. B. 1995. *Dusk of Dawn: An Essay Toward an Autobiography of a Race Concept*. New Brunswick: Transaction Publishers.

———. 2007, 1903. *The Souls of Black Folk.* Oxford & New York: Oxford University Press.

———. 1935. *Black Reconstruction.* New York: Harcourt Brace.

Dworkin, Ronald. Nov. 10, 1977. "Why Bakke Has No Case." *New York Review of Books.*

Evan, William M. 1964. "On the Margin: The Engineering Technician." *In The Human Shape of Work: Studies in the Sociology of Occupations,* Peter L. Berger, ed., 83–112. New York: Macmillan.

Eze, Emmanuel. 2001. *Achieving Our Humanity: The Idea of the Postracial Future.* Hoboken: Taylor and Francis.

Farr, James. 2008. "Locke, Natural Law, and New World Slavery." *Political Theory* 36(4): 495–522.

Feagin, Joe R. 1991. "The Continuing Significance of Race: Antiblack Discrimination in Public Places." *American Sociological Review* 56(1): 101–6.

———. 2006. *Systemic Racism: A Theory of Oppression.* New York: Routledge.

Feagin, Joe R., and Melvin P. Sikes. 1994. *Living with Racism: The Black Middle-Class Experience.* Boston: Beacon Press.

Feagin, Joe R., and Robert Parker. 1990. *Building American Cities: The Urban Real Estate Game.* Englewood Cliffs, NJ: Prentice Hall.

Feinberg, Joel. 1980. *Rights, Justice, and the Bounds of Liberty,* Princeton, NJ: Princeton University Press.

Finkelman, Paul. 2001. "Slavery and the Constitutional Convention: Making a Covenant with Death." In *Slavery and the Founders: Race and Liberty in the Age of Jefferson,* Paul Finkelman, ed., 3–36. New York: M. E. Sharpe.

———. 2003. *Defending Slavery: Proslavery Thought in the Old South.* Boston: Bedford Books.

Fireside, Harvey. 2004. *Separate and Unequal: Homer Plessy and the Supreme Court Decision That Legalized Racism.* New York: Carroll & Graf Publishers.

Fiss, Owen. 1976. *Groups and the Equal Protection Clause. 5 Phil. & Pub. Aff.* 107.

Fourie, Carina. 2011. "What Is Social Equality? An Analysis of Status Equality as a Strongly Egalitarian Ideal." *Res Publica* 18: 107–26.

Franklin, John Hope. 1963. *The Emancipation Proclamation.* New York: Doubleday.

Fredrickson, George M. 1971/2008. *The Black Image in the White Mind: The Debate on Afro-American Character and Destiny, 1817–1914.* New York: American Council for Learned Societies.

Fricker, Mranda. 2007. *Epistemic Injustice: Power and the Ethics of Knowing.* Oxford & New York: Oxford University Press.

Galenkamp, Marlies. 1998. *Individualism versus Collectivism: The Concept of Collective Rights.* Rotterdam: Sanders Instituut: Gouda-Quint.

Gardiner, Burleigh, and William F. Whyte. 1945. "The Man in the Middle: Position and Problems of the Foreman." *Applied Anthropology* 4(2): 1–28.

Glazer, Nathan. 1975. *Affirmative Discrimination, Ethnic Inequality, and Public Policy.* Cambridge, MA: Harvard University Press.

Gold, Michael E. 2001. *An Introduction to the Law of Employment Discrimination,* 2nd ed. Ithaca: Cornell University Press.

Goldberg, Chad Allen. 2012. "Robert Park's Marginal Man: The Career of a Concept in American Sociology." *Laboratorium* 4(2): 199–217.

Goldberg, Milton M. 1941. "A Qualification of the Marginal Man Theory." *American Sociological Review* 6(1): 52–58.

Gotanda, Neil. 1995. "A Critique of 'Our Constitution Is Color-Blind.'" In *Critical Race Theory: The Key Writings That Formed the Movement,* 257–75. New York: The New Press.

Gould, Stephan Jay. 1981/1996. *The Mismeasure of Man.* New York: W. W. Norton & Co.

Graham, Howard Jay. 1968. *Everyman's Constitution: Historical Essays on the Fourteenth Amendment, The "Conspiracy Theory," and American Constitutionalism.* Madison: Wisconsin Historical Society Press.

Grant, G. Kathleen, and Jeffrey R. Breese. 1997. "Marginality Theory and the African American Student." *Sociology of Education* 70(3): 192–205.

Graves, Joseph L., Jr. 2001. *The Emperor's New Clothes: Biological Theories of Race at the Millenium*. New Brunswick, NJ: Rutgers University Press.

Green, Robert P. 2000. *Equal Protection and the African American Constitutional Experience*. Westport, CT: Greenwood Press.

Greene, Linda S. 1990. "Race in the 21st Century: Equality through Law?" 64 *Tul. L. Rev.* 1515.

Griffin, Paul R. 2000. *Seeds of Racism in the Soul of America*. Naperville, IL: Sourcebooks.

Haney-Lopez, Ian. 2006. *White by Law: The Legal Construction of Race*. 10th Anniv. Ed., New York and London: New York University Press.

Harris, Cheryl I. 1993. "Whiteness as Property," 106 *Harv. L. Rev.* 1707.

Hickman, Christine B. 1997. "The Devil and the One-Drop Rule: Racial Categories, African Americans, and the U.S. Census." 95 *Mich. L. Rev.* 1161.

Higginbotham, A. Leon, and Barbara K. Kopytoff. 1989. "Racial Purity and Interracial Sex in the Law of Colonial and Antebellum Virginia." 77 *Geo. L.J.* 1967.

Hilfiker, David. 2003. *Urban Injustice: How Ghettos Happen*. New York: Seven Stories Press.

Ho, A. K., et al. 2011. "Evidence for Hypodescent and Racial Hierarchy in the Categorization and Perception of Biracial Individuals." 100 *J. of Personality & Soc. Psychol.* 492.

Hobbes, Thomas. 1651. *Leviathan*. Penguin Books.

Hoffman, Frederick L. 1896/2004. *Race Traits and Tendencies of the American Negro*. Clark, NJ: Lawbook Exchange.

Hoy, David Couzens. 1985. "Interpreting the Law: Hermeneutical and Poststructuralist Perspectives." *Southern California Law Review* 58: 136–76.

———. 1987. "Dworkin's Constructive Optimism v. Deconstructive Legal Nihilism," *Law and Philosophy* 6: 321–56.

———. 1992. "Intentions and the Law: Defending Hermeneutics." In *Legal Hermeneutics: History, Theory, and Practice*, ed. Gregory Leyh, 173–86. Berkeley, Los Angeles, and Oxford: University of California Press.

Hubbard, Ruth, and Elijah Wald. 1999. *Exploding the Gene Myth: How Genetic Formation Is Produced and Manipulated by Scientists, Physicians, Employers, Insurance Companies, Educators, and Law Enforcers*. Boston: Beacon Press.

Hunt, Alan. 1999. "Marxist Theory of Law." In *A Companion to Philosophy of Law and Legal Theory*, ed. Dennis Patterson, 355–66. Malden, MA: Blackwell Publishing.

Irvine, William. 1955. *Apes, Angels, and Victorians: The Story of Darwin, Huxley, and Evolution*. New York: Meridian Books.

James, Joseph B. 1966. *The Framing of the Fourteenth Amendment*. Champaign: University of Illinois Press.

Jasper, Margaret C. 2008. *Employment Discrimination Law under Title VII*. Oceana's Legal Almanacs: Law for the Layperson. 2d ed. Oxford: Oxford University Press.

Jiménez, Erick Raphael. 2014. "Aristotle on Natural Slavery: The Race Question," *Graduate Faculty Philosophy Journal* 35(1–2): 53–79.

Johnson, Jr., Earl. 2009. "Equality before the Law and the Social Contract." 37 *Fordham Urb. L.J.* 157.

Johnson, Kevin R., ed. 2003. *Mixed Race America and the Law*. New York and London: New York University Press.

Johnson, Peter A. 1960. "The Marginal Man Revisited." *Pacific Sociological Review* 3(2): 71–74.

Johnston, David, ed. 2000. *Equality*. Indianapolis: Hackett Publishing Company.

Jopling, W. H. 1991. "Leprosy Stigma." In *Leprosy Review*. Mar. 62(1): 1–12.

Jordan, Winthrop D. 1968/2012. *White over Black: American Attitudes toward the Negro 1550–1812*. Chapel Hill: University of North Carolina Press.

———. 2014. "Historical Origins of the One-Drop Rule in the United States." *Journal of Critical Mixed Studies* 1(1): 98–132.

Kant, Immanuel. 2000. "Of the Different Human Races." In *The Idea of Race,* Robert Bernasconi and Tommy L. Lott, eds., 8–22. Indianapolis/Cambridge: Hackett Publishing Company, Inc.

Karst, Kenneth L. 1989. *Belonging to America: Equal Citizenship and the Constitution*. New Haven: Yale University Press.

Kennedy, Stetson. 1990. *Jim Crow Guide: The Way It Was*. Boca Raton: Florida Atlantic University Press.

Klarman, Michael J. 2004. *From Jim Crow to Civil Rights: The Supreme Court and the Struggle for Racial Equality*. New York: Oxford University Press.

Kluger, Richard. 1975. *Simple Justice: The History of* Brown v. Board of Education *and Black America's Struggle for Equality*. New York: Knopf.

Korgen, Kathleen Odell. 2016. *Race Policy and Multiracial Americans*. Bristol: Policy Press.

Kull, Andrew. 1992. *The Color-Blind Constitution*. Cambridge, MA, London: Harvard University Press.

Larson, Edward. 2006. *Summer for the Gods: The Scopes Trial and America's Continuing Debate over Science and Religion*. New York: Basic Books.

Lawrence, Charles R., III. 1995. "The Id, the Ego, and Equal Protection: Reckoning with Unconscious Racism." In *Critical Race Theory: The Key Writings that Formed the Movement*, 235–57. New York: The New Press.

Lawson, Bill E. 1992. *The Underclass Question*. Philadelphia: Temple University Press.

———. 1995. "Living For the City: Urban United States and Environmental Justice." In *Faces of Environmental Racism,* L. Westra and P. Wenz, eds., 41–55. Lanham, MD: Rowman & Littlefield.

———. 2008. "The Value of Environmental Justice." *Environmental Justice* 1(3): 155–58.

Lebron, Christopher. 2015. *The Color of Our Shame: Race and Justice in Our Time*. New York: Oxford University Press.

Leong, Nancy. 2010. "Judicial Erasure of Mixed-Race Discrimination," 59 *Am. U. L. Rev*. 469.

Lewontin, R. C. 1972. "The Apportionment of Human Diversity." *Evolutionary Biology* 6: 381–98.

Leyh, Gregory, ed. 1992. *Legal Hermeneutics: History, Theory, and Practice*. Berkeley, Los Angeles, Oxford: University of California Press.

Lieber, Francis. 1880/2010. *Legal and Political Hermeneutics*. Lawbook Exchange, Ltd.

Livingstone, Frank B. 1962. "On the Nonexistence of Human Races." *Current Anthropology* 3: 279–81.

Lovejoy, Arthur O. 1942. *The Great Chain of Being: A Study in the History of an Idea*. Cambridge, MA: Harvard University Press.

Lucas, Lauren Sudeall. 2014. "Undoing Race? Reconciling Multiracial Identity with Equal Protection." 102 *Calif. L. Rev*. 1243.

Lundmark, Thomas. 2008. *Power & Rights in U.S. Constitutional Law,* 2nd ed. Oxford and New York: Oxford University Press.

MacKinnon, Catharine A. 1987/1994. *Feminism Unmodified*. Cambridge, MA: Harvard University Press.

Marx, Karl. 1843/1994. "On the Jewish Question." In *Karl Marx, Selected Writings,* ed. Lawrence H. Simon, 1. Indianapolis & Cambridge: Hackett Publishing Company, Inc.

———. 1859/1994. Preface to *A Contribution to the Critique of Political Economy*. In *Karl Marx, Selected Wrtitings,* ed. Lawrence H. Simon, 209. Indianapolis & Cambridge: Hackett Publishing Company, Inc.

———. 1967. *Capital. A Critical Analysis of Capitalist Production,* Vol. 1. New York: International.

Marx, Karl, and Friedrich Engels. 1846/1994. "The German Ideology." In *Karl Marx, Selected Writings*, ed. Lawrence H. Simon, 209. Indianapolis & Cambridge: Hackett Publishing Company, Inc.

Matsuda, Mari. 1995. "Looking to the Bottom: Critical Legal Studies and Reparations." In *Critical Race Theory: The Key Writings that Formed the Movement*, eds. Kimberlé Crenshaw, Neil Gotanda, Garry Petter, and Kendall Thomas. New York: The New Press.

May, Larry. 1987. *The Morality of Groups: Collective Responsibility, Group-Based Harm, and Corporate Right*. Notre Dame: University of Notre Dame Press.

McCormack, Thelma Herman. 1956. "The Druggist's Dilemma: Problems of a Marginal Occupation." *American Journal of Sociology* 61(1): 308–15.

McGary, Howard. 1999. "Racial Integration and Racial Separatism: Conceptual Clarifications." In *Race and Social Justice*, Howard McGary, ed., 43–61. Malden, MA: Blackwell Publishers Inc. Originally published in *Philosophy Born of Struggle*, Leonard Harris, ed., 199–211. Kendall/Hunt Publishers, 1983.

———. 1999. *Race and Social Justice*. Malden, MA: Blackwell Publishers, Inc.

McIntosh, Peggy. 2008. "White Privilege: Unpacking the Invisible Knapsack." In *Women, Images and Realities: A Multicultural Anthology*, 388–92. New York: McGraw-Hill Companies [reprint from 1988 working paper].

McKerlie, Dennis. 2001. "Aristotle's Theory of Justice." *The Southern Journal of Philosophy* 39(1): 119–41.

Miller, David. 1998. "Equality and Justice." In *Ideals of Equality*, Andrew Mason, ed., 21–36. Oxford: Blackwell.

Mills, Charles. 1997. *The Racial Contract*. Ithaca and London: Cornell University Press.

———. 2005. "Ideal Theory as Ideology." *Hypatia* 20(3): 165–84.

———. 2007. "Equality." In *Toward a New Socialism*, Anatole Anton and Richard Schmitt, eds., 75–98. Lanham, MD: Rowman & Littlefield Publishers, Inc.

———. 2009. "Critical Race Theory: A Reply to Mike Cole." *Ethnicities* 9(2): 270–81.

———. 2014. "Notes from the Resistance: Some Comments on Sally Haslanger's *Resisting Reality*." *Philosophical Studies* 171(1): 85–97.

———. 2015. "Racial Equality." In *The Equal Society: Essays on Equality in Theory and Practice*, George Hull, ed., 43–71. Lanham, MD: Lexington Books.

Montagu, M. F. Ashley. 1942. *Man's Most Dangerous Myth: The Fallacy of Race*. New York: Columbia University Press.

Mootz, Francis J., III. 1988. "The Ontological Basis of Legal Hermeneutics: A Proposed Model of Inquiry Based on the Work of Gadamer, Habermas, and Ricoeur." 68 *B.U.L. Rev.* 523.

———. 1994. "The New Legal Hermeneutics." 47 *Vand. L. Rev.* 116.

Murray, Charles. 1984/2015. *Losing Ground*. New York: Basic Books.

Murray, Charles, and Richard J. Herstein. 1996. *The Bell Curve*. New York: The Free Press.

Myrdal, Gunnar. 1944/1996. *An American Dilemma: The Negro Problem and Modern Democracy*. New Brunswick, NJ: Transaction Publishers.

Nash, Al. 1978. "The University Labor Educator: A Marginal Occupation." *Industrial and Labor Relations Review* 32(1): 40–55.

Nudd, T. Roger. 1961. "The Dean is a Marginal Man." *Journal of Educational Sociology* 35(4): 145–51.

Nussbaum, Martha 2000. *Women and Human Development: The Capabilities Approach*. Cambridge: Cambridge University Press.

Oliver, Melvin. 1980. "The Enduring Significance of Race." *Journal of Ethnic Studies* 7(4): 79–91.

Oliver, Melvin L., and Thomas M. Shapiro. 1995/2006. *Black Wealth/White Wealth: A New Perspective on Racial Inequality*. New York: Routledge.

Omi, Michael, and Howard Winant. 1994. *Racial Formation in the United States*. New York: Routledge.

Onwuachi-Willig, Angela. 2013. *According to Our Hearts*. New Haven and London: Yale University Press.

Outlaw, Lucius. 1997. "Conserve Races? In Defense of W.E. B. Du Bois." In *W.E.B. Du Bois on Race and Culture*, ed. Bernard W. Bell, 15–37. New York and London: Routledge.

———. 2005. *Critical Social Theory in the Interests of Black Folks*. Lanham, MD: Rowman & Littlefield.

Packard, Jerrold M. 2002. *The American Nightmare: The History of Jim Crow*. New York: St. Martin's Press.

Park, Robert E. (May) 1928. "Human Migration and the Marginal Man." *The American Journal of Sociology* 33(6): 881–93.

Pashukanis, Evgeny. 2007. *A General Theory of Law and Marxism*. New Brunswick and London: Transaction Publishers.

Pateman, Carol. 1988. *The Sexual Contract*. Stanford: Stanford University Press.

Patterson, Dennis. 1996/1999. "Postmodernism." In *A Companion to Philosophy of Law and Legal Theory*, ed. Dennis Patterson, 375–84. Malden, MA: Blackwell Publishing.

Perea, Juan F. 1997. "The Black/White Binary Paradigm of Race: The 'Normal Science' of American Racial Thought." 85 *Calif. L. Rev.* 123.

Piper, A. 1992. "Passing for White, Passing for Black." *Transition* 58: 5–32.

———. (Fall–Spring) 1992–1993. "Xenophobia and Kantian Rationalism." *Philosophical Forum* 24(1–3): 188–232.

Rawley, James A. 1989. *Turning Points of the Civil War*. Lincoln: University of Nebraska Press.

Rawls, John. 1971. *A Theory of Justice*. New Delhi Universal Law Publishing Co. Ltd.

———. 1996. *Political Liberalism*. New York: Columbia University Press.

Raz, Joseph. 1986. *The Morality of Freedom*. Oxford: Clarendon.

Record, Jane Cassels. 1957. "The Marine Radioman's Struggle for Status." *American Journal of Sociology* 62(4): 353–59.

Reid, Margaret. 1982. "Marginal Man: The Identity Dilemma of the Academic General Practitioner." *Symbolic Interaction* 5(2): 325–42.

Rivera, Amaad, Jeannette Huezo, Christina Kasica, and Dedrick Muhammad. 2009. *State of the Dream 2009: The Silent Depression*. Boston: United for a Fair Economy.

Rives, Scot. 2011. "Comment: Multiracial Work: Handling Over the Discretionary Tool of Multiracialism, 5 *UCLA L. Rev.* 1303, 1309.

Rockquemore, Kerry Ann, and David L. Brunsma. 2002. "Socially Embedded Identities: Theories, Typologies, and Processes of Racial Identity among Black/White Biracials." *Sociological Quarterly* 43(3): 335–56.

Rothstein, Richard. 2017. *The Color of Law: A Forgotten Historoy of How Our Government Segregated America*. New York: Liveright Publishing, a division of W. W. Norton & Co.

Root, Maria P. P. 1995. "The Multiracial Contribution to the Psychological Browning of America." In *American Mixed Race: The Culture of Microdiversity*, 231–36. Oxford: Rowman & Littlefield Publishers.

Saks, Eva. 1988. "Representing Miscegenation Law." *Raritan* 8(2): 39–69.

Scalia, Antonin. 1997. *A Matter of Interpretation: Federal Courts and the Law: An Essay*. Princeton, NJ: Princeton University Press.

Scheffler, Samuel. 2015. "The Practice of Equality." In *Social Equality: On What It Means to Be Equals*, Carina Fourie, Fabian Schuppert, and Ivo Wallimann-Helmer, eds., 21–44. New York: Oxford University Press.

Schnapper, Eric. 1985. "Affirmative Action and the Legislative History of the Fourteenth Amendment." 71 *Virginia Law Review* 5: 753–98.

Schwartz, Bernard. 1973. *From Confederation to Nation: The American Constitution, 1835–1877*. Baltimore: Johns Hopkins University Press.

Sealing, Keith E. 1999–2000. "Blood Will Tell: Scientific Racism and the Legal Prohibitions Against Miscegenation." 5 *Mich. J. Race & L.* 559.

Sears, Nathaniel C. 1920. *Abraham Lincoln, Politician and Patriot: An Address*. Chicago: Union League Club.

Segesvary, Victor. 1995. "Group Rights: the Definition of Group Rights in the Contemporary Legal Debate based on Socio-Cultural Analysis." *International Journal on Group Rights* 3(2): 89–107.

Shelby, Tommie. 2005. *We Who Are Dark: The Philosophical Foundations of Black Solidarity*. Cambridge, MA: Belknap Press of Harvard University Press.

Sheth, Falguni. 2009. *Toward a Political Philosophy of Race*. Albany, NY: SUNY Press.

Shipman, Pat. 1994. *The Evolution of Racism: Human Differences and the Use and Abuse of Science*. New York: Simon and Schuster.

Spencer, Quayshawn. 2012. "What 'Biological Racial Realism' Should Mean." *Philosophical Studies* 159(2): 181–204.

Spickard, Paul R. 1989. *Mixed Blood: Intermarriage and Ethnic Identity in Twentieth-Century America*. Madison, WI: University of Wisconsin Press.

Stanton, William Reagan. 1960. *The Leopard's Spots: Scientific Attitudes toward Race in America, 1815–59*. Chicago: University of Chicago Press.

Squires, Gregory D. 1994. *Capital and Communities in Black and White: The Intersections of Race, Class, and Uneven Development*. Albany: State University of New York Press.

Stephens, Otis H., Jr., and John H. Scheb II. 2007. *American Constitutional Law Volume II: Civil Rights and Liberties*. Belmont, CA: Thomson Wadsworth.

Stonequist, Everett V. 1937. *The Marginal Man; A Study in Personality and Culture Conflict*. New York: Russell & Russell.

Sullivan, Shannon. 2006. *Revealing Whiteness: The Unconscious Habits of Racial Privilege*. Bloomington: Indiana University Press.

Sullivan, Shannon, and Nancy Tuana, eds. 2007. *Race and Epistemologies of Ignorance*. Albany, NY: SUNY Press.

Sundstrom, Ronald R. 2008. *The Browning of America and the Evasion of Social Justice*. Albany: State University of New York Press.

Sweet, Frank W. 2005. *Legal History of the Color Line: The Rise and Triumph of the One-Drop Rule*. Palm Coast, FL: Backintyme.

Takaki, Ronald T. 1990. *Iron Cages: Race and Culture in 19th Century America*. Oxford: Oxford University Press.

Taylor, C. C. W. 1995. "Politics." In *The Cambridge Companion to Aristotle*, Jonathan Barnes, ed., 233–58. Cambridge: Cambridge University Press.

Taylor, George H. 2000. "Hermeneutics and Critique in Legal Practice: Critical Hermeneutics: The Intertwining of Explanation and Understanding as Exemplified in Legal Analysis." 76 *Chi.-Kent L. Rev.* 1101.

Taylor, Paul C. 2004. *Race: A Philosophical Introduction*. Cambridge: Polity.

Thernstrom, Stephan, and Abigail M. Thernstrom. 1997. *America in Black and White: One Nation, Indivisible*. New York: Simon & Schuster.

Thomas, Brook, ed. 1997. Plessy v. Ferguson: *A Brief History with Documents*. Boston: Bedford Books.

Trefousse, Hans. 1969. *The Radical Republicans: Lincoln's Vanguard for Racial Justice*. New York: Alfred A. Knopf.

Tribe, Laurence. 1988. *American Constitutional Law*. Mineola, NY: The Foundation Press.

UNESCO. 1951. *Race and Science: The Race Question in Modern Science*. New York: Columbia University Press.

Wadlington, Walter. 1966. "The Loving Case: Virginia's Anti-Miscegenation Statute in Historical Perspective." 52 *Va. L. Rev.* 1189.

Wallenstein, Peter. 1994. "Race, Marriage and the Law of Freedom." 70 *Chi.-Kent L. Rev.* 371.

Waller, James. 2001. *Prejudice Across America*. Jackson: University of Mississippi Press.

Wardwell, Walter I. 1952. "A Marginal Professional Role: The Chiropractor." *Social Forces* 30(3): 339–48.

Warner, Richard. 1996/1999. "Legal Pragmatism." In *A Companion to Philosophy of Law and Legal Theory*, ed. Dennis Patterson, 385–93. Malden, MA: Blackwell Publishing.

Weisberger, Adam. 1992. "Marginality and its Directions." *Sociological Forum* 7(3): 425–46.
West, Robin. 1990. "The Meaning of Equality and the Interpretive Turn." 66 *Chi.-Kent. L. Rev.* 451.
Westen, Peter. 1990. *Speaking of Equality*. Princeton, NJ: Princeton University Press.
Williams, Kim M. 2006. *Mark One or More: Civil Rights in Multiracial America*. Ann Arbor, MI: University of Michigan Press.
Williams, Patricia J. 1995. "Alchemic Notes: Reconstructing Ideals from Deconstructed Rights." In *Critical Race Theory: The Key Writings that Formed the Movement*, eds. Kimberlé Crenshaw, Neil Gotanda, Garry Petter, and Kendall Thomas. New York: The New Press.
Wolfsdorf, David. 2017. "Morality and Aristotelian Character Excellence." In *Questions of Character*, Iskra Fileva, ed., 19–32. New York: Oxford University Press.
Woodburn, J. A. 1913/2017. *The Life of Thaddeus Stevens: A Study in American Political History, Especially in the Period of the Civil War and Reconstruction*. London: Forgotten Books.
Woodward, C. Vann. 1967/2006. *The Strange Career of Jim Crow*. 3rd rev. ed. New York: Oxford University Press.
Wray, Donald E. 1949. "Marginal Men of Industry: The Foremen." *American Journal of Sociology* 54(4): 298–301.
Yancy, George. 2017. *Black Bodies, White Gazes: The Continuing Significance of Race*, 2d. ed. Lanham, MD: Rowman & Littlefield.
Yoshino, Kenji. 2011. "The New Equal Protection." 124 *Harv. L. Rev.* 747.
Zack, Naomi. 1993. *Race and Mixed Race*. Philadelphia: Temple University Press.
———. 1994. "Race and Philosophic Meaning." *APA Newsletter on Philosophy and the Black Experience* 94(1): 14–20.
———. 2002. *Philosophy of Science and Race*. New York: Routledge.
———. 2010. "The Fluid Symbol of Mixed Race," *Hypatia*, 25th Anniversary Issue, 25(4): 875–90.
Ziller, R. C., B. J. Stark, and H. O. Pruden. 1969. "Marginality and Integrative Management Positions." *The Academy of Management Journal* 12(4): 487–95.

CASES

Adarand Constructors, Inc. v. Peña, 515 U.S. 200 (1995).
Alexander v. Holmes County Board of Education, 396 U.S. 19 (1969).
Brown v. Board of Education, 347 U.S. 483 (1954).
Brown v. Board of Education II, 349 U.S. 294 (1955).
City of Richmond v. J.A. Croson Co., 109 S.Ct. 706 (1989).
(The) Civil Rights Cases, 109 U.S. 3 (1883).
Defoe v. Spiva, 625 F.3d. 324 (6th Cir. 2010).
Dred Scott v. Sanford, 60 U.S. 393 (1857).
Frontiero v. Richardson, 411 U.S. 677 (1973).
Fullilove v. Klutznick, 448 U.S. 448 (1980).
Gratz v. Bollinger, 539 U.S. 244 (2003).
Green v. Franklin National Bank, 459 F.3d 903 (8th Cir. 2006).
Grutter v. Bollinger, 539 U.S. 306 (2003).
Hernandez v. Texas, 347 U.S. 475, 74 S.Ct. 667 (1954).
Korematsu v. United States, 323 U.S. 214 (1944).
Loving v. Virginia, 388 U.S. 1 (1967).
Madison v. IBP, Inc., 330 F.3d 1051 (8th Cir. 2003).
Martin v. Wilkes, 490 U.S. 755 (1989).
McLaurin v. Oklahoma State Regents, 339 U.S. 637 (1950).
Memphis Firefighters v. Stotts, 467 U.S. 561 (1984).
Missouri ex rel. Gaines v. Canada, 305 U.S. 337 (1938).

Ozawa v. United States, 260 U.S. 178 (1922).
Pace v. Alabama, 106 U.S. 583 (1883).
Plessy v. Ferguson, 163 U.S. 537 (1896).
Regents of the University of California v. Bakke, 438 U.S. 265 (1978).
(City of) Richmond v. J.A. Croson Company, 488 U.S. 469 (1989).
Sheet Metal Workers v. Equal Employment Opportunity Commission, 478 U.S. 421 (1986).
Sipuel v. Oklahoma Board of Regents, 332 U.S. 631 (1948).
(The) Slaughterhouse Cases, 83 U.S. 36 (1873).
State v. Brown, 108 S.E.2d 233, 234 (La. 1959).
Strauder v. West Virginia, 100 U.S. 303 (1880).
Sweatt v. Painter, 339 U.S. 629 (1950).
United States. v. Bhagat Sing Thind, 261 U.S. 204 (1923).
United States v. Carolene Products, 304 U.S. 144 (1938).
United Steelworkers v. Weber, 443 U.S. 193 (1979).
Wards Cove Packing Co. v. Antonio, 109 S.Ct. 2115 (1989).
Washington v. Davis, 426 U.S. 229 (1976).
Wheaton v. North Oakland Medical Center, 130 Fed.Appx. 773 (6th Cir. 2005).

STATUTES

Acts of West Virginia 1872–1873.
Article 2404 of the Louisiana Civil Code.
Civil Rights Act of 1866, 14 Stat. 27–30 (1866).
Civil Rights Act of 1875, 18 Stat. 335–337 (1875).
Civil Rights Act of 1964, Pub. L. 88–352, 78 Stat. 241 (1964).
Tex.Const., Art. VII, §§ 7, 14; Tex.Rev.Civ.Stat. (Vernon, 1925), Arts. 2643b (Supp. 1949), 2719, 2900.
The Three-fifths Clause of the U.S. Constitution (1787).
Virginia's Racial Integrity Act of 1924.
U.S. Const. amend. XIV. Passed June 13, 1866, ratified July 9, 1868.

Index

About the Author

Tina Fernandes Botts is assistant professor of philosophy at California State University, Fresno. She is also an attorney. Her research areas are philosophy of law, philosophy of race, feminist philosophy and hermeneutics. She is the editor of *Philosophy and the Mixed Race Experience*, 2016, Lexington Books, the co-author, with Rosemarie Tong, of the fifth edition of *Feminist Thought*, 2017, Routledge, the author of peer-reviewed philosophy journal articles in *Res Philosophica, Philosophy Today, The Journal of Applied Ethics and Philosophy,* and *Critical Philosophy of Race,* as well as numerous book chapters, including chapters in *The Oxford Handbook of Philosophy and Race,* Naomi Zack, editor, Oxford University Press, 2016, *Race Policy and Multiracial Americans,* Kathleen Korgen, editor, Policy Press, 2016, and *The Routledge Companion to Hermeneutics,* Jeff Malpas and Hans-Helmuth Gander, editors, Taylor and Francis, 2014. She is also the former chair of the American Philosophical Association's Committee on the Status of Black Philosophers.

www.ingramcontent.com/pod-product-compliance
Lightning Source LLC
LaVergne TN
LVHW090413210926
848480LV00002B/556